Sam Gardener

NOTES FROM A COLD CLIMATE ANTARCTIC SYMPHONY (SYMPHONY NO. 8)

Notes from a Cold Climate

COMPOSER TO TRAWL FROZEN WASTES FOR ANTARCTIC SEQUEL

Antarctic Symphony (Symphony No. 8)

SOUND OF SILENCE INSPIRES ANTARCTIC SINFONIA

Notes from a Cold Climate

Antarctic Symphony (Symphony No. 8)

Notes from a Cold Climate

MAX GOES
FOR
SYMPHONY
ON ICE

Antarctic Symphony (Symphony No. 8)

First published in
the United Kingdom, April 2001,
by Browns/London.
First edition – 1,500 copies.
Designed by Browns/London.

Browns
29 Queen Elizabeth Street
London SE1 2LP
United Kingdom

Telephone +44 (0)20 7407 9074
peter@brownsdesign.com
www.brownsdesign.com

ISBN 0-9533730-3-7

Printed in Holland by Chevalier.
Paper supplied by Trebruk UK.
Pages 01-12 and 57-152 printed
on Arctic Extreme 150gsm.
Pages 13-56 printed on
Munken Pure 70gsm.

Acknowledgements
Antarctic trek inspires symphony
The Daily Telegraph 17.06.97

*Composer to trawl frozen wastes
for Antarctic sequel*
The Scotsman 17.06.97

*Sound of silence inspires
Antarctic sinfonia*
The Guardian 17.06.97

Max goes for symphony on ice
Birmingham Post 05.08.97

Photographs©
British Antarctic Survey, NERC
High Cross
Madingley Road
Cambridge CB3 0ET
United Kingdom

Telephone +44 (0)1223 221 400
www.antarctica.ac.uk

Philharmonia Orchestra
1st Floor
125 High Holborn
London WC1V 6QA
United Kingdom

Telephone +44 (0)20 7242 5001
www.philharmonia.co.uk

Antarctic Symphony
(Symphony No. 8)
by Sir Peter Maxwell Davies,
for orchestra.

World Première Sunday 6 May 2001
at the Royal Festival Hall, London
by the Philharmonia Orchestra.
Conducted by
Sir Peter Maxwell Davies.

Instrumentation:
Piccolo, two flutes, two oboes,
Cor Anglais, two clarinets in A,
bass clarinet in Bb, two bassoons,
double bassoon, four horns in F,
three trumpets in C, three trombones,
tuba, percussion (four players)*,
timpani,** celesta, harp, strings.

*xylophone, glockenspiel, marimba,
crotales, tubular bells, bell tree,
very small high wood block,
tambourine, side drum, two bass
drums (small, very large), Chinese
cymbals, clashed cymbals, four
suspended cymbals (very small,
small, medium, large), nipple gong,
tam-tam (with plastic soapdish),
tuned brandy glasses (with water),
two small pebbles, football rattle,
biscuit tin (filled with broken glass),
three lengths builders' scaffolding
(small, medium, large).

**with Japanese temple gong
and two cymbals.

Diary©
Sir Peter Maxwell Davies
c/o Judy Arnold
50 Hogarth Road
London SW5 0PU
United Kingdom

www.maxopus.com/

11 **Commissioning the symphony**
Introduction by Linda Capper,
British Antarctic Survey

13 **Notes from a Cold Climate**
The diary of Sir Peter Maxwell Davies

57 **The inspiration**
Photographs by Pete Bucktrout

142 **Britain in the Antarctic**
The work of British Antarctic Survey

143 **Philharmonia Orchestra**

143 **Sir Peter Maxwell Davies**
Essay by John Warnaby
Chronological list of published works
Curriculum vitae

Antarctic Symphony (Symphony No. 8)

Notes from a Cold Climate

Commissioning the symphony

Antarctica – the frozen continent. An enigmatic expanse of awe-inspiring beauty. A land where there are no native people. A continent devoted to peace and science, where scientists from around the world unravel the mysteries of our Earth – it is a unique natural laboratory.

In 1948 the Ealing Studios film *Scott of the Antarctic*, starring Sir John Mills, captured the world's imagination. The film score, composed by Ralph Vaughan Williams and performed by the Philharmonia Orchestra, evoked the heroism, failure and eerie silence of Antarctica. Vaughan Williams went on to develop the score into the first Antarctic Symphony, *Sinfonia Antartica*, which was performed in 1953 by the Hallé Orchestra, conducted by Sir John Barbirolli in Manchester. In the audience that night was a young Peter Maxwell Davies.

Over 50 years later British Antarctic Survey (BAS) and the Philharmonia Orchestra commissioned Sir Peter Maxwell Davies to write a sequel to the work that was, for so many people, an introduction to one of the most fascinating regions of our Earth.

This commission was an opportunity for both BAS and the Philharmonia to experiment in an innovative way to fuse science with music. Who better to commission than a man who has a strong commitment to the environment – a composer whose work is of 'place' whether writing about Orkney, where he lives, or Antarctica. The emotions are stirred and the listener engaged memorably. Sir Peter Maxwell Davies' *Antarctic Symphony (Symphony No. 8)* is his last. Through it, a whole new generation will be introduced to scientific excitement through a creative work that somehow communicates the concept of Antarctica's global importance in understanding issues like ozone depletion and climate change.

In 1997 Sir Peter Maxwell Davies accepted an invitation from BAS to obtain firsthand experience and inspiration for the new symphony. For a month he lived with scientists and support staff onboard the Royal Research Ship *James Clark Ross* and at Rothera Research Station on the Antarctic Peninsula. To stand on the deck of *James Clark Ross* as she sailed through the frozen sea, ice crashing and banging the hull, thrilling everyone onboard, passing icebergs with the bluest of blue gashes lighting their interiors was an incredible experience that Vaughan Williams could have only dreamed of.

This book records Sir Peter Maxwell Davies' fascinating journey through his diary entries. Share the composer's thoughts, impressions and inspiration. Read about his dramatic journey and the conversations he enjoyed with biologists and glaciologists. Imagine how he felt when left alone to camp in a pyramid tent with a field assistant on the heart-stoppingly beautiful Jones Ice Shelf. Throughout his journey BAS photographer Pete Bucktrout captured these moments for posterity – the pictures in this book give you a glimpse of a unique Antarctic experience.

The discovery of the Antarctic ozone hole by BAS scientists in 1985 changed the world by alerting us to the damage wrought on our atmosphere by chemical pollutants. Perhaps Sir Peter Maxwell Davies' *Antarctic Symphony* will change the way we think of the frozen continent.

Linda Capper
British Antarctic Survey

Notes from a Cold Climate

Notes from a Cold Climate
The diary of Sir Peter Maxwell Davies

The whole story of my going to the Antarctic began when my manager, Judy Arnold, in the course of one of our conversations said, *"By the way, I had this call from the Philharmonia Orchestra, who put me in touch with the British Antarctic Survey in Cambridge, and there's this idea, that they might like you to write this Antarctic Symphony to mark the 50th anniversary of the Vaughan Williams'* Sinfonia Antartica, *and the music he composed for the film* Scott of the Antarctic".

I was more and more grabbed by the idea, and thought that this was going to be tremendous fun...

Sir Peter Maxwell Davies

Antarctic Symphony (Symphony No. 8)

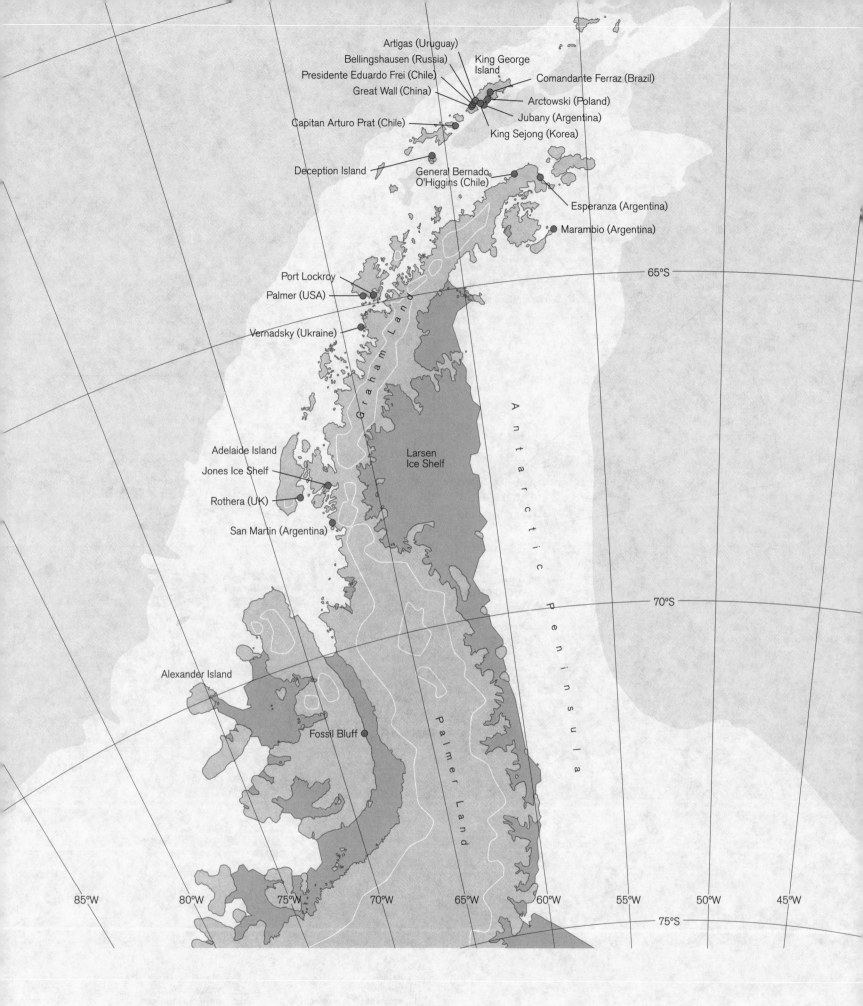

Artigas (Uruguay)
Bellingshausen (Russia)
King George Island
Presidente Eduardo Frei (Chile)
Comandante Ferraz (Brazil)
Great Wall (China)
Arctowski (Poland)
Jubany (Argentina)
Capitan Arturo Prat (Chile)
King Sejong (Korea)

Deception Island
General Bernado O'Higgins (Chile)

Esperanza (Argentina)
Marambio (Argentina)

65°S

Port Lockroy
Palmer (USA)

Graham Land

Vernadsky (Ukraine)

Antarctic Peninsula

Adelaide Island
Jones Ice Shelf
Larsen Ice Shelf
Rothera (UK)

San Martin (Argentina)

70°S

Alexander Island

Palmer Land

Fossil Bluff

85°W   80°W   75°W   70°W   65°W   60°W   55°W   50°W   45°W

75°S

Monday 15.12.97
On board a late morning British Midland flight from Edinburgh to Heathrow –
my ideal kind of flight,
blissfully smooth,
with few enough passengers,
so that you can clutter the next two seats with papers,
while a friendly staff plies you with abundant free alcohol.
Wonder about the next flight, tonight,
from Brize Norton, Oxfordshire, courtesy of the RAF,
down to the Falkland Islands –
vague forebodings of military discipline and style.
And the next leg,
by ice-strengthened boat from there to the Antarctic –
I have signed my life away for five days,
declaring that I shall Obey the Master in All Things.
Nervous laughter at the thought of three days' physical training and
life-preservation instruction at Rothera,
the main UK Research Station in the Antarctic.
In preparation for living in a tent in the 'field' –
nagging memories of *Scott of the Antarctic*,
the film whose music, by Vaughan Williams,
and the symphony he later fashioned out of it,
I am meant to be celebrating in a work of my own,
commissioned by the British Antarctic Survey (BAS) in Cambridge,
and the Philharmonia Orchestra, London.
This is no usual composer's commission –
part of the deal is that I have to embrace the Antarctic in fact.
When you sign a contract for a piece of music,
the reality of writing it is still two years or more away:
now I have to face up to an intimidating and probably hilarious reality,
as the Antarctic materialises with a vengeance.
Faded long memories of incompetence in gym classes at school resurface,
along with a chilling recall of my lack of skill,
tolerated by commander and fellow islanders,
co-opted as a ten-year auxiliary coastguard on Hoy, Orkney.

Everyone has been saying how life on Hoy will have hardened and prepared
me for proximity to the South Pole.
Nonsense.
I shall crave the warmth of the stove,
the presence of books,
musical scores,
compact discs,
the home bread-maker,
fresh fruit,
the wine-rack,
garlic –
but, hardly think such excuses would convince anyone if I turn back now.

Antarctic Symphony (Symphony No. 8)

Tuesday 16.12.97
Collected at Heathrow by Judy Arnold, my manager,
and driven to Oxford,
where we spent the afternoon with the Woodgates,
a retired professor of atomic physics and his wife –
old friend from the Dartington Summer School of Music.
Judy was not going to be left out of this adventure,
and, even though we're both over 60,
by which time one is strictly no longer eligible for employment by
the British Antarctic Survey,
we passed all the compulsory medical tests,
and are left now, over cups of soothing tea and wadges of comforting cake,
to regret our foolhardiness.
Talk about anything but the adventure to come,
with lots of rather forced, hollow hilarity.

Brize Norton –
all sinister floodlights in the freezing darkness,
with vaguely intimidating military protocol –
rigorous filling in of forms, issue and showing of passes.
Queue for check in with Falkland Islanders returning home for Christmas –
they manhandle vast amounts of excess luggage,
looking remarkably like Orcadians and Shetlanders checking in at Aberdeen –
the same gestures, clothes, facial expressions.
Feel somehow a little comforted by this –
a tad less fish out of water.
RAF Tristar –
more legroom than in your usual commercial cattle-class stall,
but with tacky-looking ad-hoc repairs,
in fat strips of silver sticky tape, to any damaged seats,
and reading lights that refuse to work.
Ah well, a good excuse to try to sleep.
The stewards efficient and friendly,
though you feel it would be very unwise indeed to cross them.

After eight hours of flying through darkness,
arrival at Ascension Island –
25°C,
the heat hitting you like a blowtorch as you descend the airplane steps.
Barked at like a recruit by an RAF-type, to take off your sun-hat –
an unexplained bit of military lore.
We are herded into a huge mesh enclosure,
part roofed over, part open, and padlocked in,
while ordered not to take photographs.
The airfield is hideous with the brutal scarring of landscape and the whine
of stationary jet-planes.
Dark volcanic lava, with surreal white antennae,
dishes and spheres superposed.
Everyone takes photographs.
In the distance a most appealing mountain,
its summit forever appearing from and disappearing into cloud,
with what look from here like oak trees along its ridge.
Perhaps a life would be possible in Ascension after all,
out of sight and sound of the air base,
beyond that magic mountain.

The last part of the flight to Mount Pleasant, Falkland Islands,
we are accompanied by a pair of RAF Tornado Fighters,
parallel at each wing-tip –
magnificent and disconcerting.
In the queue for immigration Judy and I,
along with Julian Paren, assistant to the director of British Antarctic Survey,
are called away to a VIP lounge,
where an army officer makes apologies –
they knew we were on the flight only two minutes before,
so there's no coffee, and no limousine to take us into Stanley –
but our luggage is brought out specially,
and our passports dealt with while we sit in easy chairs.
Eventually we carry our bags to join the other 33 BAS members,
already waiting on the bus.

Drive through an immense lunar landscape,
with outcrops of rock-like pale dragons' backs,
jagged hills sticking up abruptly.
Light, luminous greys shot with purple and pink.
Names familiar from the 1982 war –
Tumbledown, Wireless Ridge, Mount Harriet.
Along the road are frequent signs displaying skull and crossbones,
with the word MINEFIELD.
The mines, it seems, will never be removed –
it would cost too much.
Some beaches near Port Stanley are mined,
and due to shifting sands cannot adequately be cleared –
there is a great resentment still at this.
As you enter Stanley there's a Thatcher Drive,
and further along a monument to thank the liberators –
all strangely moving in this context,
a town not even as big as Stromness in Orkney.

The Royal Research Ship (RRS) *James Clark Ross* sits in the harbour,
partly painted a strident red,
looking curiously unfathomable and impregnable,
bristling with cranes, gear, complexity.
She is the BAS ice-strengthened ship which will take us down to Rothera,
the main British Antarctic base –
this should take five days or so,
though we are threatened with a possible air ferry for the last section –
Rothera is ice-bound,
with the sea ice beginning to break.

A splendid cabin all to myself on the Bridge Deck –
net plastic wadding already in place on surfaces,
bars across open shelves, in readiness for heavy seas.
A reassuring welcome from the master, Chris Elliott.

Wednesday 17.12.97

A day of sightseeing, courtesy of the organisation 'Falklands Conservation' –
gentoo penguins above Bertha's Beach,
in a stately group of 70 or so,
feeding their young, squabbling,
some offering a mate a present of a small piece of stone or carefully selected
fragment of wood.
One magnificent solitary king penguin standing slightly aloof,
observing calmly.
As a newcomer to penguins, outside the zoos of childhood,
I'm surprised they are so undisturbed by a few humans crouching so close,
clicking and whirring away,
and then amazed at the Jekyll and Hyde routine,
when they enter and leave the sea –
on land performing a slightly comic balancing dance on tail and splayed feet,
with outstretched rudimentary wings working on overdrive,
and in the water a lethal torpedo,
an arrow of deadly speed and power.
At Gypsy Cove the magellanic penguins stand sentinel before their burrows,
with another huge congregation on the shore,
meditating before or after feeding in the sea.
Evidence, in collapsed burrows,
of sea-lions taking the chicks.
Becky, our guide, is extraordinarily skilled at the wheel,
driving us over bumps, tussocks and rocks,
speaking volumes for the preferred vehicle here –
the old-fashioned Land Rover,
which takes enormous punishment, and which you can still repair yourself.
The beaches infinite windswept white,
alive with petrels, sandpipers, plovers.
Winds merciless and chill –
balaclavas, gloves, scarves, layers of thick wool.
Turkey vultures, with black crooked wings,
like a secret and sinister military plane:
military starlings, with red fronts.
A paradise for birdy folk –
indeed there are special bothies for them on the outer isles,
which Falklands Conservation encourages them to visit.

Dinner at Government House with the Governor, H.E. Richard Ralph.
Pleasantly unstuffy –
a fine building, partly mid-nineteenth-century, with three-foot thick walls,
all in the process of sympathetic restoration.
Scottish view from the flower-filled conservatory over the harbour –
a scene heartachingly peaceful.
The retainer who serves me a gin and tonic relates how he survived in the house
when the Argentinians took over,
of corpses in the garden.
James Peck, a Port Stanley artist who just exhibited his Falklands war paintings
in Buenos Aires, tells of the sympathetic reaction to his work in Argentina.
A great joy to see Tom Eggeling and Megan –
the former planning officer for Orkney,
now working here;
she is a former stalwart of the St. Magnus Festival in Orkney.
Full of admiration for the courage of such a move relatively late in one's career.

Thursday 18.12.97
Breakfast aboard RRS *James Clark Ross* –
so many scientists, consuming full English breakfast,
with a kipper option,
beneath huge signed photographs of the Queen and Prince Philip.
The Queen launched the vessel on Tyneside in 1990 –
must have been one of the last such shipbuilding undertakings.

The widening gap between the ship and shore:
departure by boat is the archetype of that experience.
Here it expresses perfectly the finality of the Antarctic's onset –
no opportunity, now,
to change one's mind, and jump ship.
The bridge is a roomful of discreet controls and computer displays.
Chris the captain manoeuvres us through the Narrows:
Port Stanley fades.
A gentle swell,
cold sun,
giant petrels and small albatrosses circle.
With Linda Capper and Pete Bucktrout,
make the first tapes for radio and television coverage of the trip.

An hour-long drill on safety and survival,
which includes wearing life-jackets,
boarding and strapping ourselves in a lifeboat,
and learning how to operate the watertight doors deep in the ship's bowels –
those doors which separate the vessel into different compartments,
to prevent flooding throughout, in case of holing.
Felt distanced,
as from every marine disaster movie.
Imagination refused to contemplate the fumbling, ashen reality.

Antarctic Symphony (Symphony No. 8)

Friday 19.12.97
Up on the bridge at 2.00am to see the recovery of an oceanographic device
which had been gathering information at the bottom of the sea for a year.
Its precise whereabouts are well recorded,
and the 'capture' is plotted, eventually with satellite help.
The whole procedure takes a couple of hours,
as we slow down and close in:
the two-thirds waxing moon sheds enough light,
together with on-deck illumination,
to dramatise the lurches of the sea and foam smashing over the fore-deck,
out of all proportion to the relatively mild bucking of the boat.
The hushed bridge,
controls and computer screens flickering in the dark,
emanates a tight sense of tense urgency.
Once located, the device is automatically released,
and takes about 20 minutes to surface from a depth of only 1,000 metres or so.
Julian is the first to spot its flashing light –
in a laboratory on lower deck its radio signal is monitored –
and captain Chris and Robert Paterson hold
and gently control the dancing ship.
Grappling irons appear on deck, and the round object,
over one metre across and a metre deep, bristling with apparatus,
is winched on board.
We return to our cabins in a grey-white, bruised-blue dawn,
to sleep as we may until we gather again at 7.30am for a full breakfast of egg,
bacon and sausage.

The ordinary morning rituals of showering,
shaving and dressing demand hitherto unknown skills.
The boat was heaving all manner of which-ways,
trying to make the floor vertical in wild, uncharted directions.
No cupboard or room door could be left open, unless locked.
Open – it crashes back, probably knocking you over with stunning aim.
Any item, like a shaving gel canister or a deodorant stick,
flies through the air with a will of its own.
In the shower, you learn to hold on with one hand and soap with the other,
or wedge yourself against the wall,
while water squirts all around as from a demented hose-pipe.
You aim a foot at a sock and fall off the chair to spread-eagle across the
shuddering floor.

Judy, my manager, spends almost all the time in her cabin.
This is a pity –
she would have loved videoing the oceanographic recovery mission,
and now the seabirds swooping parallel to the boat –
we are well down in albatross regions.
Sea and sky a brutal iron grey.
The wind whistles from the north, already cold and slappy enough.

Linda, a keen bird-watcher,
was sending an e-mail to the British Antarctic Survey in Cambridge,
and was unable to finish,
overtaken by a sudden seasickness.
A few moments later an e-mail came back,
alerting her to a particular kind of albatross, to be seen out of the porthole.

The wonders of modern science –
BAS has a programme to track the albatrosses by satellite,
as their movements are still shrouded in mystery.
This specimen, at that moment,
was trailing on the computer screen in Cambridge,
exactly parallel to us, starboard side.
Linda left much cheerier upon being able to confirm the sighting.

The thrill,
the childish sense of pure, innocent wonder,
looking out and seeing one's first iceberg.
This one looks as if the Sydney Opera House has broken moorings
and gone AWOL.

Saturday 20.12.97
A procession of icebergs,
mysterious and deeply awe-inspiring.
Of course it is we who are moving faster,
but in calmer waters one has the illusion of a stately mannequin parade,
as the model's outlines modulate,
revealing new and secret shapes and colours.
Contours suddenly glow with an iridescent blue of an unimaginable intensity:
this is the best exhibition of abstract sculpture I ever saw.
All that one has read of fractals and the Mandelbrot set floods the brain,
perhaps as some kind of bulwark against the wonder,
which I quietly admit is overwhelming,
even transcendental.
Some icebergs pick up and maintain the upward surge of wave motion;
some repeat and develop the forms of clouds;
others, seen against a backdrop of snow-covered cliffs and hills,
take up the forms and energies characteristic of these;
while the best combine all of these features with a capricious dynamism
that constantly modifies and transforms as we pass.
A whale,
travelling at a furious 15 knots, faster than the ship,
briefly surfaces,
its back confirming a neighbouring iceberg.
Another iceberg suddenly appears as a gigantic swan.
Another reveals a Norman arch, 50ft high,
with ice packed above this for another 100ft –
a broken-off fragment of a medieval abbey.

Sometimes I find mealtime conversation quite baffling –
top scientists talk shop,
their jargon bristling with acronyms.
They are very patient when I enquire about their particular speciality
and any possible future practical application.

Monday 22.12.97
The engines stop,
and 33 scientists, Judy and I file down a rope ladder into a launch
already bulging with boxes, barrels, crates.
We are delivering supplies to the tiny station of Port Lockroy,
and dropping off Dave Burkitt and Rod Downie who will man the place
alone for three months.
It was established in 1944, and abandoned in 1962.
In 1996 it was restored by the U.K. Antarctic Heritage Trust,
and now boasts a small museum and post office,
to open in summer for visits by cruise ships and private yachts.

The pack ice has broken up enough for us to land without problems –
a very small, rocky island,
with gentoo penguins nesting everywhere,
so that you must take great care not to disturb them, right away upon beaching.
The smell of penguin guano crinkles your nose –
all-pervasive bad fish.
Everybody carries the cargo into the store-shed or up to the house:
each case is clearly marked, and checked on a tally by Dave,
who semaphores the operations.
The privilege of raising the British flag to the top of its mast,
at the highest point by the house,
falls to Linda, on behalf of BAS, and me.
Such an unaccustomed honour makes me very nervous,
as I fumble with intransigent ropes,
tugging ineffectively and desperately.
A great relief when the flag ascends and unfurls.

A magical spot,
an island surrounded by mainland cliffs, monumental white mountains.
The all-pervasive sound is of broken pack-ice lifting on and off the shore rocks –
a gargantuan cocktail shaker.
Add to that the gentle buzz of conversation among the ubiquitous penguins,
with the occasional raised squawk as a sheathbill –
a small grubby white seabird –
lunges towards a penguin egg,
and that's the island's sound spectrum.

The mainland is only 100 yards away from one point,
but safety regulations determine that the keepers are not allowed to have a boat.
Their accommodation is sparse but solid –
there is plenty of coal still from the forties –
and the museum has relics evocative of that time –
ancient cans of food, oatmeal packets, tools *in situ*,
all with excellent explanatory displays.

Once we have determined that the radio link to the main station
at Rothera is operative,
we pile back into the launch and return to the RRS *James Clark Ross*.
This was the first time I had worn any of the Antarctic gear issued by BAS –
it was surrealistic being kitted out at headquarters in Cambridge last July,
pulling on layer after layer of thermals and waterproofs on one of the
hottest days ever –
but here we would not survive without these.

It is a great relief to take them off for lunch –
particularly the huge guano-smeared boots.
There are strict dress codes for meals on board,
to be transgressed at one's peril.

This afternoon we glide through the Lemaire Strait –
a narrow passage between the almost vertical sides of mountains jutting
thousands of feet up into cloud.
Apart from the gentle hum of the boat's engines,
the *JCR* is extremely quiet, to facilitate very precise sonar experiments –
the silence is profound.
There is hardly any talk, either, on the bridge or on deck –
everyone is so over-awed by the grandeur,
the power of the unfolding spectacle.
My words can give no suggestion of the self-transcendence invoked,
and I fear, too,
that any music I eventually write can only give the palest hint.
One of the most serendipitous moments came when a snow avalanche poured
and billowed down the mountain directly to starboard –
imagine the mightiest, gentlest,
longest whisper ever –
we were enveloped in mad, dancing flakes,
a white-out –
a moment that will last a lifetime.

Shortly after 4.00pm a small party descended a very long rope ladder into
a very small launch,
to take Christmas mail to Vernadsky,
the Ukrainian Antarctic Expedition base.
This base was formerly British,
named Faraday after Michael Faraday the physicist,
and was handed over to the Ukrainians in 1995.
John Harper, the mate of the *JCR*, was in charge,
standing tall at the stern,
shouting instructions and semaphoring to the wheel-house,
to ensure a safe passage through the ice-flows.
Even the unfrozen sea-water was like oil,
thickly viscous.
A gaggle of long huts on a small rise, where we tie up,
welcome enthusiastically,
and we are helped through deep snow to the Christmassy domestic warmth
of the settlement.
Such a joyful, beautiful welcome from the dozen or so men and women –
we take off our boots and layers of gear,
and troop up to the bar.
This is the biggest and most famous bar in the Antarctic –
a riot of decorative carving,
made by over-enthusiastic British joiners, who,
for the waste of time and wood,
were promptly sent home.

Delighted hosts and guests,
excellent black coffee of the kind that dissolves the spoon and scalds your tonsils,
chocolate,
generous globes of Ukrainian cognac.

A welcoming speech from Vladimir Okrugin, the head of the team,
and we are shown round the base by Svetlana,
a meteorologist, climbing champion, guitarist and computer expert.
Many things –
equipment, notices, photographs –
have been left as they were when the British ran the station.
Up a ladder into a loft office,
where we met Daphne, a Dobson spectrophotometer,
the piece of scientific equipment, from 1957,
which was the means of discovering the hole in the ozone layer.
A speech by Julian Paren,
generous vodka all round,
stirring Ukrainian music,
and we are bobbing our way through corridors of ice back to the
RRS *James Clark Ross*.
A huddle of figures waving on the jetty:
one wonders when anyone will visit them next.
Pete Bucktrout, our official photographer,
asks why all international and diplomatic relations can't be like this.
Why indeed?!
I sport the badge of the Ukrainian Antarctic Expedition,
and clutch a book about their homeland.

Tuesday 23.12.97
A final day on the RRS *James Clark Ross*,
of a splendour to outshine even these extraordinary days.
We ploughed through the ice fields in brilliant sunshine,
wrapped up on deck in our windproof multi-layers,
any exposed skin liberally smeared with anti-sun goo.
Everyone balaclavaed and anonymous behind intensely black BAS issue goggles
with essential black side-flaps –
sea ice and distant snowy peaks thrust millions of crystal needles into any
unprotected eyes.

Disconcerting,
in the infinite silence hushing the hundreds of gleaming square miles around us,
to hear ice crack and split before the bow,
then roar along keel to the stern in a tumultuous clatter of slabs and shards.
Even more unnerving to hear this ice break,
and feel the judder and grind, deep inside the hull.
Several of us were treated to a guided tour of the ship's bowels.
The GEC engine, made in Rugby.
The thrusters.
The biological filtration system for sewage.
The stabilisers.
The water supply, to which calcium must be added to modify its purity.
Everything operating theatre clean – no dust, no grease,
though I would hate to have to effect repairs,
with so much packed as small as possible,
wires and tubes at crazy angles,
disappearing into the difficult spaces.
This must be the most advanced and well-kept research vessel there is.

At midnight I was still up on the top deck,
in brilliant sunshine,
watching for occasional penguins and huge seals to flip gently off the ice,
out of the boat's way.
In a huge stretch of unfrozen sea,
a sudden pod of minke whales, spouting,
leaping and pirouetting out of the water.

The ice is sometimes several feet thick:
it would have stopped any other boat.
Eventually we park for the rest of the white night,
before starting engines at 6.00am,
for the final approach,
and our delicate, tricky berthing at Rothera Research Station.

Paul Rose, the base commander, comes on board to greet us
and give a pep talk about safety on the base.
No smoking indoors.
Gear.
Boot rooms.
Gash duty.
Training.
Behaviour in the field.
He is so enthusiastic you feel a nagging guilt about harbouring any fears
or doubts at all.

Wednesday 24.12.97
A day spent on radio interviews,
and getting to know my temporary home.
In winter there are 20 or so people here –
in summer the number jumps to over 100,
and one senses that the original 20 subliminally resent the incomers...
The base loud with tractors and general clangour.
As the RRS *James Clark Ross* is unloaded,
the compressed waste is loaded, for landfill near Port Stanley.

The setting magnificent,
man's contribution stark and unlovely –
a barracks of a place.
In another incarnation it could be a penal boot camp.
I share a tight room with two others –
there are four bunks, two by two, facing the door,
with a small window between the bunks, directly opposite the door.
I am designated (MAXWELL P) the top left bunk.

Twenty years ago, after the ultimate drunkard,
snorer and sweaty socks experiences in railway sleepers,
I vowed never again to share accommodation with strangers.
However, I persuade myself this is all in a good cause,
and for the good of my soul –
here are some of the world's top scientists,
sharing with intrepid engineers, pilots, medics, cooks, –
a whole support team –
so what kind of wimp am I?
(I later discover that the acoustic properties of the building amplify any
snore or fart from distant 'pitrooms',
and when the fellow in the lower berth innocently turns over,
the whole world resonates tinnily through the metal tubes of the bunk.)
Toilet and showering facilities are communal –
horrible memories of compulsory sport at school.
I suppose, in such a base, with a heavy British Military hangover,
this is supposed to produce male bonding of the approved sort.
(There are women here, but you feel they must somehow fit themselves in:
if they became pregnant they'd be sent home.)
This is all in stark contrast to the Chilean base,
where I'm told there are families with children,
a small school, and a more ordinary civilian atmosphere.
However, I can well understand the British –
one must take care where there is such a high risk of accidents,
what with vehicles, machines, air traffic so close by,
the fire hazard of wooden and plastic building, laboratories –
not to mention the perils of ice and snow.
I am given a 'laboratory' for my work –
a sideways extension of a corridor,
where doors bang open and shut and prepossessed people rush by demonically.
I am very privileged to have such a space to myself –
everyone else has to share.

Eventually the rock music pulsing through the thin walls drives me to join
Judy, my manager, with her computer,
plus Linda, BAS publicity officer, with hers,

plus Julian, assistant to BAS Director, Cambridge,
and Pete Bucktrout, with his mountain of photographic gear heaped up,
in a windowless cubicle of a 'laboratory',
where the incessant tramping across the ceiling,
the clamour of voices from all around and about,
and the noises of machinery are preferable.
Sudden subversive thoughts of an anti-Antarctic Symphony,
featuring the antiphonal bleeps, revs, roars and skids of frenzied vehicles,
a scherzo caricaturing broody scientific boffins on closely adjacent nests,
based on Vaughan Williams' penguins,
and a grand finale featuring myself as an automaton on speed hanging on to the
phone through dozens of frantic publicity interviews to Britain and elsewhere.

But, but, but... one has only to glance outside to put all this in proportion.
The sky is a dizzy blue,
the intensity of the whiteness is breathtaking.
It dwarfs into insignificance our best efforts to trivialise and brutalise the
landscape –
at least thus far,
so long as the International Antarctic Treaty of 1959 holds.
This is reinforced by a flight around the immediate environs –
the base looks tiny, neat, even pretty,
with its grey building and sculptured dishes, domes,
and antennae from far up on high,
and the wonders of the land and seascape occupy the attention absolutely
(as we step from the twin otter, base reality takes over again –
pop music floods the whole station,
resonating between cliffs and sea, with the hangar acting as loudspeaker).

Everyone is taking enormous trouble to accommodate a person the likes of
whom they would normally never encounter.
The whole Rothera team appears to perform in cheerful harmony –
hardworking and loyal.
I am allocated a minder, or 'general assistant', Rachel Duncan –
a young lady so energetic, fulfilled, radiant,
healthy that again I feel such a wimp,
imagining her rescuing me from cliff ledges and crevasses,
or scolding me gently for putting my tent up incorrectly.

Sunday 28.12.97
Spent a morning in the new Bonner Laboratory,
learning about algae, lichens, moss etc. –
much emphasis on the causes and results of global warming and ozone depletion,
as regards Antarctic wildlife with implication for life everywhere on the planet.
David Wynn-Williams, a leading scientist here,
showed us the small 'greenhouses' –
a foot wide, two long, which are set up on field site,
with either ultra-violet opaque or UV-transparent perspex,
either with or without walls,
to manipulate and observe the effects of radiation in different ways;
experiments are conducted in the field and in the laboratory to observe the
results of an estimated 3°C rise in temperature by 2050.
There is a laudable, exemplary awareness of and sensitivity to the fragility of
certain polar environments –
some areas are not allowed to be interfered with at all,
for fear of destroying them,
others are to be touched only most carefully,
while a few are designated for heavy research.
We were shown controlled environment cabinets (CECs),
for experiments with and observations on photosynthesis, humidity,
carbon dioxide presence in the atmosphere etc.
As genuine sunlight cannot be simulated in these CECs,
experiments exposing microbes to the worse-case scenario of ozone deprivation
will be conducted on a space shuttle shortly.

We discussed the ominous polar amplification factor in relation to global warming –
when a little ice melts in response to a small rise in temperature,
the surface of the ground is exposed,
which heats up in the warmer atmosphere as it never did while under the ice,
which in turn affects and melts adjacent ice,
starting an ongoing meltdown,
out of all proportion to the initial small temperature rise.
(The main continent of Antarctic ice is isolated still by the surrounding ocean,
and is mostly between 6,000ft and 12,000ft thick,
but a change in ocean currents could eventually trigger off melting here,
with globally catastrophic results.)
The one species of Antarctic grass, *Deschampsia Antarctica*,
is spreading alarmingly already –
it is suggested this, too, is due to regional warming.
The scientists are very proud of their Bentham spectrum radiometer,
with a bundle of light filters,
that sees the UV change, and plots this second by second.

The equipment for microbiology must be absolutely sterile –
any impurity or foreign organism whatsoever is fatal.
There is a freezer, for instance, which stores material at -80°C –
a low enough temperature to preserve chlorophyll –
also most impressive dark and illuminated incubators for moss etc.

A small compound microscope, connected to a computer,
measures micro-organisms in soil –
every detail of their position, distribution, volume, weight, diameter,
all you need to know about each thread, nodule –
and everything about the surrounding soil.

This is invaluable in terms of UV radiation effects –
one can observe micro-organisms, either through the lens or on the screen,
magnified 1,000 times.
In a soil core at extreme Antarctic conditions,
cells can grow at 10 units of light,
as opposed to 18,000 units of sunlight:
there are even endolithics – extremely simple organisms,
that live up to 10 millimetres down in the coldest Antarctic rock –
which have the slowest metabolic rate I have ever heard of:
they take 10,000 years to transform a minuscule amount of carbon dioxide
into proteins etc.
What a lifespan, and what a life!
Will this have some implications for the time structures in the new
Antarctic Symphony?!

Ron Lewis Smith is a plant ecologist specialising in moss and lichen –
he is particularly interested in the effects of UV radiation (UVB) change,
along with temperature rise, moisture availability, etc.
on hitherto unvegetated ground,
with the implications for growth and reproduction cycles.
We see a wonderful array of specimens from Charcot Island,
a newly discovered site with a most varied spectrum of plant life.
Again, it is the shapes of the lichens which are fascinating,
their growth lines, dynamism, modulations:
perhaps I identify too readily with the old-fashioned 'pathetic fallacy',
but they do open up whole worlds of design and form –
memories of D'Arcy Thomson's volume on *Growth and Form* avidly read
as a supplement to arid school biology.
Ron also talks about mites, nematode worms and tardigrades,
and how these survive extremely low temperatures.
Nematode worms,
for instance, are the most successful and populous animal in Antarctica –
they produce eggs which contain a very large proportion of anti-freeze.
There are even small concentrates of lichen,
measured in millimetres,
over 6,000ft above sea level,
and, most interestingly in relation to increasing UVB levels,
there is a common black moss here on Rothera Point which contains,
naturally,
pigmentation to screen out any harmful radiation.

A walk around Rothera Point takes you into a world light-years away from base.
The silence is as absolute as possible,
the sight of sea ice, icebergs, distant snow-covered mountains,
rocks with algae and moss,
snow still covering some of the rock,
part tinged green and rose with snow-algae,
all just heart-rendingly beautiful.
I did a very strange interview for the BBC television programme
The Weather Show, in which I talked with John Turner,
the British Antarctic Survey's senior meteorologist.
Felt extremely stagy.
Selected bits of rock for Eric Guest and John Rothera, as requested,
at the top of the hill by the wooden cross –
a monument to people who died while serving here.

Odd how Eric, who must be my oldest friend,
was talking to John Rothera, one of his oldest friends,
and at whose wedding he was best man,
just before I phoned him to tell him that I was coming to Rothera.
I had no idea that this base was named after this John Rothera,
who did cartography in the early days.

A splendid mulled wine party,
hosted by Chris Elliott, on board his vessel the *JCR,*
on Christmas Eve.
All on base and all the *JCR* crew present –
plenty of room on the after deck for all,
now that unloading was well under way.
Cold enough, but brilliant sunshine –
everyone quite merry and loud.
Christmas carols discreet in the background floating from discreet loudspeakers.
My last chance to see quite a lot of the crew I had grown to rely on, respect,
and even like these last days.

Peter B is staying in accommodation worse than mine –
a very small cubicle, with no window.
This office where the five of us work also has no window,
and is overheated –
you have to leave the door open.
(They claim here that it is more fuel-economical to constantly overheat
the base than to regulate the heating.)

Christmas Day.
A traditional dinner, with all the usual stuff.
Compliments to Nigel the chef.
Laddish behaviour all round:
the presence of a family element would mitigate that.
(This office is as difficult as the corridor base I abandoned –
constant conversation, constant huge thudding of feet on the ceiling,
sound from the giant video machine upstairs in the dining room,
usually hollerin' football crowds,
and pop music from the gym next door.)

Boxing Day.
A trip by snow-cat along the ridge of snow above Rothera, below the ski run.
Except that the snow-cat, driven by Ian Marriot,
got stuck:
there are new crevasses, down which it seems we could easily have plunged –
the fore starboard caterpillar lunged into a crack and almost spilled us.
Ian reversed the snow-cat gingerly up and out and back,
while we continued until the base was out of sight and sound,
Rachel prodding the snow constantly for crevasses.
A good walk –
lots of loud cracking of ice and rock and a rushing of snow and scree from the
rock-face above –
and a wonderful outlook over the frozen sea.
The ridge is now, due to the crevasses,
officially out of bounds, until further notice.
Ian Marriot is from Bolton, with a gentle musical voice and accent:
a poet, with a lightning but quiet sense of humour.

No less than two Twin Otter aircraft to ferry me and my minder, Rachel,
to the Jones Ice Shelf,
about 15 minutes flight from Rothera.
Andy Alsop is our pilot,
Geoff Porter flies the other plane.
Andy lives in Kirkwall,
and the last time I sat in the co-pilot's seat next to him must have been
on a Loganair Islander hop to Hoy, over 20 years ago.
The other passengers are Judy, my manager;
Linda, BAS publicity and press officer;
Julian Paren;
Pete Bucktrout, BAS official photographer;
and Kurt Farkas, general field assistant.
I am filmed helping load the plane, jumping up to the co-pilot's seat, etc.
not just once, but with retakes,
until Pete and Linda are satisfied.
It is a perfect day, as we glide over black and white peaks,
and look down into cavernous gulleys,
whose bombazine blackness seems to reach down into an infinity below the
Earth's crust.

The landing is rather alarming for the uninitiated.
When landing on skis in ice and snow
one is duty-bound to test the surface for crevasses,
marking it at a first run, with engines running full,
then landing only if the ice is deemed firm and smooth enough.
We touch down within inches of a giddy, blue crevasse in the ice shelf.

There is little time to take in the surroundings,
except to notice that we are ringed by craggy mountains and glaciers.
I know we are on a floating expanse of ice,
trapped in this location,
20 yards or more thick,
which is expected to break up and drift away within the next
100 years or so.
I am filmed helping unload the plane, and setting up the tent –
this is embarrassing,
as I'm a novice, and have to be carefully rehearsed.
The bright orange-red tent is eventually up and firmly anchored to the ice,
the ground-sheet laid,
the boxes of provisions, medical aid, etc.
in their regulation positions,
the sleeping bags set up,
the Tilley between them on its platform in order,
the radio working,
and, at last, the planes take off,
leaving me alone with Rachel, my minder.

Then, a real silence, in glorious sunshine,
with the Heim and Anteus glaciers to the north,
where the scene is totally dominated by the huge bulk of Mt. Rendu;
to the south-east the Bader and Bucker glaciers,
Mt. Kershaw and the Koshiba Wall;
and to the south-west Blaiklock Island,
Mt. Arronax and Mt.Verne, on Pourquoi Pas Island.

All these place names are new to me,
and it is only because Julian pointed them out just before he took off that
I remember them at all.
Many features of the landscape commemorate explorers and others who
rendered good service in the Antarctic,
while many names are unexpected and far-fetched.
A range of features by the Larsen Ice Shelf is tagged with characters in
Melville's *Moby Dick,*
while on Alexander Island, there's a rag-bag of musical composers.
I feel with respect that these are not real names –
they haven't been lived,
and have no significant and specific human associations or resonances,
and could, frankly, be interchanged.
A few names are good enough –
Mt. Kershaw itself commemorates a pilot who was killed and buried at its foot,
and Fossil Bluff gives a fair foretaste of that place –
but most seem less permanent,
even, than those squares and streets called after politicians in France or Italy,
which changed according to the political climate.
In sum,
some of these Antarctic names lack the numen and magic associated with
real place names.
This does not imply that all these Antarctic places themselves lack
numen and magic,
which is of a very different order to that of even the remotest place in Europe.
It is the absence of mankind and his ugly baggage that enables one to enjoy,
here, on the ice shelf,
the impressions of ear and eye totally uncorrupted by mechanical and
electronic sound pollution,
or the occluding mists of industrial dust and gaseous waste.

The cliff faces are alive with the crack of ice,
the whoosh of tumbling snowdrift,
the rustle and clatter of falling scree.
Occasionally there is a really startling boom,
reminiscent of the one o'clock cannon above Edinburgh's Princes Street –
or an even more spine-tingling deep, deep gong stroke
as a small geological event changes the landscape just one iota,
in the course of its eternal metamorphosis.
There is almost no wind,
but occasionally an astonishing sound whistles gently from the peaks
to the south,
almost subliminal at first,
but growing into an alto-flutish lament that resonates somewhere
between your ears,
then reveals its true origin when a high and complex counterpoint,
suggesting ghostly oriental flutes,
creates a sonorous wandering difference –
tone, softly pulsing across the whole ice shelf.
The towering, very close pinnacles of rock,
with deep clefts,
must engender this phenomenon,
to which any little local breeze adds the whirr of ice splinters,
scuttling across the shelf's surface, displaced by your mukluks,
each step a dry scrunch in crystal sugar.

There are long gashes,
some many hundreds of feet,
where snow and rockfall have scooped the mountainside –
gigantic clawstrokes.
Above, the peaks form monumental, sharp, jutting triangles,
and within these are multiple smaller triangles –
within these, again, criss-crossing outlines,
but always maintaining proportions, lesser triangles:
it is often difficult to make out which are outlines defining a peak or eminence
and which are just cracks and splits within these shapes.
(In contrast, the low hill directly south-east is worn to a hump by
glacial erosion –
it looks, with its yellow-red-brown stains in the snow,
like the slag heap by a long-abandoned mine.)
Across the triangles of the mountains,
crevasses make curvy undulating crossway gashes –
a mighty contrasting repeated rhythm,
taken up and developed right across the ice shelf,
where loose, light snow blows into crystal outlines,
whose contour floats somewhere between that of cloud, and that of crevasse.
As the sun moves lower,
the crevasses in snow on Mt. Rendu make an illusory ripple effect,
implying the motion of a choppy sea,
magnified hugely and freeze-dried instantly.
The sun's position also affects patterns in those sections of glacier closest
to the frozen sea –
the crevasses merge,
and slowly blend into a stippling of dynamic cross-hatching.

It is impossible to tell where the top of the glacier ends and the cloud begins –
their colour and texture are identical at the join.
Where the glacier bulges out, magnificently,
tumbling in a frozen sweep onto the ice shelf,
it threatens with such power you subliminally feel the scouring of rock through
your boots –
hear the long scrape, as the stone is displaced.
But the time-scale of even a small displacement is more than my life-span,
its wavelength way beyond my threshold of hearing and understanding.
The sun moves even lower behind the glacier,
making a continuous line of glitter between it and me,
and as I move about,
the line follows,
the glare of ice crystals becoming as intense as the booming sun itself.

Rachel has stayed at the tent to write letters –
when I return after many hours of walking,
she cooks a regulation BAS fieldwork meal on the primus stove.
This is selected from a Manfood Box
(as distinct from a Dogfood Box of the good old days)
which contains ten days' supply for two people.
Dried curry, poured into a little boiling melted snow,
simmered for ten minutes, plus boil-in-the-bag rice.
These survival-kit meals are universally known here as 'munch',
and with lime and mango chutneys,
this one hits the spot exactly.

Eventually it is bed time, the sun still blazing.
The loo is a pit dug in the snow,
with a wall of displaced snow forming some kind of wind and modesty shield.
This arrangement, in the freezing conditions,
encourages unaccustomed speed,
but when I get back to the tent, Rachel is fast asleep.
Undressing, squirming into the sleeping-bag liner,
and the sleeping-bag itself presents dreadful problems within the extremely
limited space of the tent,
I am terrified of disturbing Rachel,
kicking over the primus, and in general causing mayhem,
as I struggle with intractable moleskins and windproofs.
Tent-sleep is the soundest, deepest, calmest yet in the Antarctic.

The design of the tent has hardly changed since Scott's day:
it is exactly right for its purpose.
It is easy to imagine living in it for months –
certainly it would take a degree of heroism to do so in the worst weather conditions,
and I realise my stay is simply unrealistic:
very well looked after,
spoiled by the best midsummer weather –
but little insight is required to understand what a field worker for BAS must endure,
and how invaluable the presence of a general assistant like Rachel must be.
I have the luxury of being able to enjoy the landscape,
and think about a symphony, in sympathetic conditions,
while they must do science in appalling circumstances,
where the smallest everyday task can become Herculean,
with inconceivable discomfort.

At seven in the morning I tentatively stick a foot out –
there are regulation ways of getting through the tent flap –
and quickly pull it back again, into the relative warmth.
It is minus something,
and I discover that last night's footprints outside the tent are hard and unyielding.
Once dressed I take a walk –
the whole feel of the ice shelf is transformed;
low cloud obscures the sun.

There is no sense of perspective at all in the blue whiteness,
and distance is impossible to judge.
The opposite rockface pushes right up to your eyeballs,
while the intervening flat snow could extend to infinity.
This, compounded by the alienation of landscape seen through the
essential snow-goggles,
makes it hard to relate even to one's own height –
feet seem to be much further down than usual.
Today's underfoot crunch is harsher, more grating.
The distant red pyramid of our tent becomes a beacon,
a reference point in the featureless ice shelf,
and a way of judging how far one has gone.
As the sun mounts, and penetrates the cloud layer to better effect,
it imparts to the high snow flanks around a platinum and silver sheen,
in places suggesting the gooey texture of giant rounds of marshmallow.
(The blackness of clefts and crags belongs to another,
quite unconnected visual dimension.)

In this lowering light, a distant glacier looks like a raging torrent.
A letterbox of cobalt blue suggests better weather to come.
Back at the tent, Rachel and I are disturbed by the sound of a plane –
there is a BAS Twin Otter plane flying over.
We think, good of them to make a little diversion to check that we're alright –
but, after circling again, the plane lands.
The weather is deemed to be deteriorating,
so that we could be stranded here for days.
Camp is quickly struck, and Rachel and I are scooped up,
back to the safety and comfort of Rothera.

That letterbox of blue expands and takes over:
the evening brings cloudless skies and the brightest sunshine,
with a gentle, tingly breeze.

I regret not having heard the air at Rothera rent by the calls of huskies;
these dogs were banned in the winter of 1993.
Even in imagination, the sound is evocative.
The last Rothera dogs were flown to Labrador,
the idea being to reintroduce there a pure strain of husky –
but the Antarctic refugees were unprotected against Canadian viruses,
and died shortly after arrival.

It was deemed wrong to have any species of animal in Antarctica not native,
which meant getting rid of all dogs.
(An exception was made for humankind.)
The 30 Rothera dogs needed 130 seals per annum for food –
these were killed over a wide area;
there are 60 million or so seals in Antarctica.
The remains not consumed by dogs were discovered by gulls and skuas,
which, encouraged also by the dumping of food waste from the Rothera kitchen,
grew unusually populous.
When dogs and dumping were banned, these gulls and skuas starved,
their population now being most dramatically reduced.

Dogs were replaced by skidoos –
small, extremely efficient vehicles, suitable for pulling sledges,
easily navigable in poor snow conditions,
and much faster than dogs.
However, they do pollute the atmosphere by burning a diesel oil and petrol mix,
and their noise is horrible.
Rothera is indeed generally extremely dependent upon fossil fuels –
there are no wind or solar power generators –
and if energy and pollution levels are ever to be reduced to 1990 levels,
as specified at the Kyoto convention,
this most difficult but worthwhile aim will have to at least be considered,
despite the comparative smallness of the station in 1990.
A small point in favour of dog teams:
when the leading dog fell into a crevasse,
the other dogs and the human driver survived.
Moreover, the dogs instinctively knew, most of the time,
where crevasses lurked beneath the snow surface,
and either refused to budge, or avoided them.
Skidoos certainly do not know,
and plunge straight down, with their human driver.

Monday 29.12.97
A Twin Otter flight to Sky-Blu and Sky-Hi –
two remote tents in the wilderness, four hours south of Rothera –
including a refuelling stop at the Fossil Bluff ski-way en route.
Anthony Tuson is our pilot:
we are flying out a geologist and his assigned general assistant to Sky-Hi,
and uplifting a pair from Sky-Blu – only 15 miles or so from Sky-Hi:
Sky-Blu will be abandoned for the present,
although the pyramid tent will remain *in situ.*

Again, I am co-pilot.
The sea ice around Rothera is fracturing.
The cracks suggest,
from up on high,
field patterns, roads, tracks, with ruined houses, chapels, byres –
these are fragments of embedded iceberg.
There are fissures which run for many miles in a straight line.
Patches of mottled ice,
where small pools of water form, black,
so that the ice-sheets look like slabs of speckled rock.
Farther south, the ice is a continuous shelf,
then there are azure pools of snow melt,
tear or kidney shaped,
scattered across its surface.
Coasts are defined by a strip of black or aquamarine water,
between frozen sea and cliff.

Striped mountains – bands of different coloured rock.
Some stripes run vertically:
one can imagine the seismic upheaval that twisted the mountain
through 90°.

At Sky-Blu there is driving snow.
It's not that it's snowing – the sky is indeed a clear pale blue! –
but the powdery snow covering the plateau whips up,
and across, and about, making landing tough,
and, once we have disembarked,
chilling us to the bone, despite warm clothing.
We warm ourselves by loading everything into the plane,
including a Nansen sledge,
and make the short hop to Sky-Hi.

Here, where the wind encourages the snow into even more furious whiplashes,
there is a unique permanent round-roofed tent –
that is, permanent until, one winter,
a storm carries it off –
for which reason it is forbidden to use it as sleeping accommodation;
pyramid tents are much more secure.
It forms a small sitting room, with a splendid Danish stove,
originally designed for the roughest conditions on fishing boats.
The space is soon toasty warm, and all six of us sit, rubbing limbs,
or stand, stamping feet, nursing scalding cups of tea and wolfing chocolate.
Many tons of chocolate disappear each year in Antarctica –
it is free, and always available,
like toothpaste, soap and suncream.

The pair picked up at Sky-Blu after weeks in the field –
a geologist and his minder –
are unshaven and ruddy,
except for white eye rings due to wearing goggles:
their eyes always seem to focus on far distances,
as they anticipate lovingly the hot food –
not 'munch'! –
and fresh fruit at Rothera,
and hot showers unlimited.
We are shown a particularly impressive geological specimen –
black rock flecked with glinting garnet.

Upon leaving, we circle to wave to the two left behind,
who stand by their red pyramid tent,
waving until they have diminished to two black dots.
They expect to see nobody for many days.

As we fly over the Monteverdi Peninsula,
Anthony tells me about mirages,
how snow and cloud can suddenly flip, and change places,
what was in the sky revealing itself to have been a cover of snow
on the ground,
and the 'snow' proving to be cloud:
I daren't even think about piloting under such conditions.
One would have thought nothing could be more intense than this
cruel glare of snow reflecting the sun,
but a line of cloud defining the coast opposite the sun is reflected
in the sea ice,
creating a dazzle more intense than anything I could have imagined:
it is simply unbearable, even for one second,
without the goggles.

Tuesday 30.12.97

At Rothera, all on base are required to participate, on a fair rotation system,
in cleaning, working in the kitchen, washing up, etc.
One such job is that of night watchman,
and I join Lloyd Peck on his tour of duty, in this capacity;
he is a distinguished marine biologist.
Basically, he ensures that fire is impossible,
particularly in the joiners' workshop, the hangar,
the travel store (camping equipment), any battery-charging installations,
the generating station, and around fuel tanks.
The high point of the tour, for me,
is going up on Rothera Point, above the base,
to note the weather,
particularly regarding cloud cover and horizontal visibility for the pilots.
From here, the view across the sea ice to distant mountains is stupendous,
and Lloyd hopes that, as it's the right time of year,
we might see killer whales teaching their offspring how to catch seals:
they flip a sheet of ice so that the seal slides into the water,
catching it, then releasing it,
so that they scramble back on to the ice.
It is tipped off again, allowing the young to catch and worry it,
and repeated again and again until the seal at last dies of its wounds.
I am quite relieved not to have to witness this.

A day out with Anya, a young seismologist, and a very competent cellist,
and Rachel, who for today is Anya's field assistant.
We are piloted by Andy, a hundred or so minutes north of Rothera,
to Pequod Glacier, above the Larsen Ice Shelf.
This is a flight of crystalline, emerald wonders.
We trail the plane's skis on a plateau of snow packed over hundreds of feet of ice,
5,000 feet up,
and eventually land smoothly enough,
into a strong head wind,
where no-one ever landed before.
Anya is quite upset we are not nearer to her experiment site –
Andy explains that he daren't land closer, on a slope,
because the wind is wrong,
so Rachel and Anya trudge off,
roped together in heavy-duty harness,
across a howling expanse of snow and ice.

They are away for well over two hours –
the red of their waterproofs gradually loses its colour,
as their size diminishes,
and they are just two jet black dots creeping across a dazzling white ridge,
behind which they eventually disappear.
Anya will download information into her laptop
about earth tremors over a period of time,
which enables her to calculate new information about thicknesses of the
Earth's crust.

The plateau upon which we stand is ringed with peaks –
so dramatic they have a hallucinatory quality,
their sharp and intensely integrated geometry having something of the surreal,
or unreal aspect of those computer-generated landscapes you see in space movies.

One peak is blackly strident under a perfectly sculpted half-sphere
of snow-covered ice –
you just cannot work out if there is a hollow under the ice,
reaching back to the mountain top,
or if the mountain top bulges out from beneath the ice:
it is alarming to feel the ice and the mountain move in their spaces,
as the eye interprets and re-interprets the visible evidence.

Andy looks concerned as the wind freshens,
and lashes the snow up around the plane's skis –
but eventually, before it becomes critical,
two black dots split the junction of dizzy white and powder blue,
slowly becoming toiling red figures,
and at last we learn of the success of Anya's findings.
On the return to Rothera, we make trial landings on ice,
with a view to establishing a place to deposit barrels
to refuel Twin Otters on flights to a proposed far-distant experimental site.

The Bonner Laboratory again,
this time to be shown the aquarium and related experiments
by its designer, Lloyd.
The analytical facilities are second to none –
there is much effort, for example,
in pollution research (gas chromatograph to examine oil in a polluted animal),
in changes in reproductive efficiency over ten years (starfish gonad analysis),
comparative metabolisms (brachiopods exhibit the lowest metabolic rate), etc.
A clam stuck with electrodes fascinates me horribly –
its heartbeat is being counted at 0°C, 3°C and 6°C
(at 6°C it is eight beats per minute);
the creature is expected to die when it cannot extract enough oxygen from the
water at about 9°C.
New to me the sea urchins, sea cucumbers,
huge sea spiders with digestive and reproductive systems in their legs,
chitons and sea-lemons:
this last is most odd, with its shell covered by a rubbery yellow mantle.
The huge sea squirts do just what you'd expect.

Friday 02.01.98
Twin Otter flight to Fossil Bluff.
My minder this time is Ian Marriot.

I had seen the station – a mile or so from the landing ski-way –
en route to Sky-Blu.
It overlooks the ice shelf,
with a great hill rearing up behind it,
and views out front to distant snow-covered mountains.
Already it reminded me of home on Hoy,
on the clifftops, with Morefea rearing up behind,
and looking out over the Pentland Firth to the mountains of Caithness
and Sutherland –
but as it was 10,000 years ago,
at the end of its last ice age.

We land on the ice, against the odds –
the conditions are deplorable,
but Andy touches down so smoothly one wouldn't notice.
Greeted by Jenny and Seamus,
meteorologist and radio operator manning the station and recording the weather,
who drag Ian and me to Fossil Bluff behind their skidoos.
We stand on the back platforms of beautiful ash sledges,
heaped with our bags,
connected to the skidoos by a short length of rope.

We rattle and bounce over lumps in the ice at 60mph –
well, perhaps 30 –
and I have never been so uncomfortable, ever.
I soon realise that you can steer the wretched sledge by leaning from side to side,
and that less rib-cage damage is inflicted if you bend your knees and crouch in
anticipation of the severest ruts and ridges.
After what felt like five hours –
it must have been all of five minutes –
we arrive,
and I try to look in possession of my senses,
as I jump ever so nonchalantly down,
ready to lug kit up the last 100 yards,
where snow and ice have melted.
Ian is not fooled –
he laughs and says he thought I was having a heart attack.
I shall wear the bruises as trophies for weeks.

The position of the station is magical –
from the surrounding verandah the views are even better than expected:
the looming hulk of hill behind enfolds and protects.
A Union Jack flutters over what is basically a one-roomed house,
which retains most of the features from 1960,
when it was built.
Four neat bunks, two by two, at one end.
A rough wooden table with four chairs.
A generous, all-dominating Raeburn.
A galley with water tank,
constantly topped up with fresh snow brought in,
steel sink, and primus stoves.

Shelves of tinned food, books, the station records,
and radio equipment.
A small bootroom,
a storeroom with chemical loo,
and a second tiny bunker-room complete the building.
A short way away, uphill, where the snow begins,
a wooden caboose mounted on a sledge, containing two bunks –
this was constructed by a member of the founder team,
who, tired of sleeping in pyramid tents,
had it dragged by dogs, along with everything else,
hundreds of miles across the ice.
It is his permanent monument.
A further storeroom and a generator, and that's it.

We celebrate Hogmanay twice – once at GMT,
then, three hours later, at midnight local time.
Jenny and Seamus cook,
the wine is Crozes Hermitage,
and there's the whisky Judy gave me.
Ian and I get on well –
he has blue eyes, the colour of an ice-melt pool,
which quiz you and laugh,
and he's built like a bullet.
His poems show great awareness of the natural world,
particularly of wild animals –
I think of Lawrence's insights in his snake poem.
An adventurer, a loner –
climbs rock-faces, dives,
does all those sporty things I'd never dream of attempting.
He's supposed to 'mind' me,
so he leads me up the shale slope behind the house,
across the ice of a decaying glacier.
Here there are crystal columns and fans,
cakestands,
armchairs of icy snow,
all speckled with the grit of constantly fragmenting rock,
and adorned with convoluted ice frills and laces,
necklaces of unimaginable intricacy and delicacy.
It's a place of hushed glory,
alive with the twinkle of falling fragments of ice,
the crisp crackle of larger splits,
the background rush of swift,
narrow water channels,
each trapped in a tight, solid conduit of white ice,
until it plunges under the shale.
It is very difficult to mount the scree slope –
no soil or vegetation binds the powdered, shattered stone,
each bootfall triggers a small avalanche, and grip is hard –
but eventually we gain a firm rock to sit upon,
and contemplate.

There is a sulky yellow-cream glow down below,
hovering above the edge of the ice shelf,
contrasting the iron-ore brown-yellow-purple rock and the painful brilliance
of snow and ice.

Notes from a Cold Climate

High above, forming and reforming around the summits,
wispy clinging grey-blue fingers.
Each individual fragment of rock an engrossing world in itself –
of stripes, layerings, mottlings, stipplings of various colours;
lumps of quartz, fossils –
of leaves, molluscs and tiny invertebrates –
scattered everywhere.
There is a fossilised forest close by –
the climate must once have been rather like south New Zealand.
I select a few shards and lumps to put on my desk
when I write the Symphony;
I had such tokens around me when I wrote *The Doctor of Myddfai*,
to help keep in touch with the spirit of the location of that opera,
a magical lake in Wales.

The next day is Ian's birthday.
Again, we celebrate with wine and whisky:
he is 30, and very sanguine about being so very old.
There is a media invasion in the late morning –
Andy brings down from Rothera the whole circus –
cameras and microphones –
together with Judy and Julian,
and I am filmed,
doing the same action, saying the same lines, *ad nauseam,*
so that it can be shot from different angles from various distances.
Eventually, after hours of this,
I refuse to be shot steering a sledge behind a skidoo.
Enough is enough.
When they have all left, Ian says,
in the sudden total hush,
"It's just like this when the in-laws have gone".

I spend a few hours walking by myself, in peace,
along the edge of the ice shelf,
up the bluff and among the ice sculptures of the dying glacier.
It would have been worth coming to Antarctica just for this.
Jenny bakes excellent bread and her pancakes are the best.

Saturday 03.01.98
Back at Rothera,
great excitement about the imminent firing,
by a team from Germany,
of a rocket, to record information about the mesosphere.
Nigel, the cook, whose chief interest is wildlife,
is really concerned about a broody skua whose nest
is very close by the launch site.
I accompany Nigel on his four-hour-long check-up of all the birds
around the point,
which he does every two days,
notebook in hand.
He examines each skua nest,
where the eggs are still unhatched,
and the two kelp gull nests,
where chicks are either imminent, or have hatched already.
I find it difficult to feel protective towards skuas,
whose population at home on Hoy increases alarmingly each year –
they are violently aggressive creatures,
dive-bombing anyone on their patch with a most alarming and
persistent determination.
Here, too, they make a squawky fuss,
and perform their usual dive-bomb act,
but Nigel ignores all of this,
and even lifts a couple of nesting birds,
ever so slightly and gently,
to check the presence and condition of the eggs.

The sea is full of ice again,
but free ice that has wandered here now the former rigid cover has split
and is part melted –
this, consisting of icebergs and floating bits,
freely comes and goes,
bunching up here,
and leaving the sea free there.
For the first time the sea smells of sea,
and there is enough open water for weddell seals to nose about,
and bask on ice floats.
Not at all discomfited by our very close approach,
they briefly open one eye,
turn over languorously,
and snore on.
Penguins wander around the rocks:
they must be very poor-sighted on land,
the way they approach and examine you, perplexed –
and extremely well-sighted under water,
to successfully hunt their prey.
An elephant seal, a long way out.
A minke whale blows and flips.
The ice is luminous to the farthest distance.
Broken sheets of it creak and moan –
polystyrene sounds,
as the sea mildly rocks and nudges them along.
Penguins on distant ice honk,
their sound carrying for miles in the stillness.

An unidentified distant whale blows.
The seals demonstrate their considerable vocabulary,
as gentle snorts,
wheezes and warbles sound from all directions.

Sunday 04.01.98

It is only now,
with the full support of British Antarctic Survey
that the likes of me can experience Antarctica.
The environment is absolutely and fundamentally hostile to our presence,
and, outside very expensive and limited specialist adventure
holiday companies,
visitors simply cannot exist.
Tourist ships only allow their customers ashore briefly,
and they are herded and supervised within small areas,
for their own well-being,
and for the sake of the environment,
and these vessels generally cannot cut through ice into the less accessible
frozen areas.
However, the polar regions have, for centuries,
been active in our imaginations,
ever since the earliest heroic explorations.
Antarctica is simply there,
weaving its history, myth, and magic into the fabric of our awareness,
and, even if few of us ever see it in fact,
it is enough to know that it exists,
just being its miraculous self.
Most of even the little I have seen and experienced must,
by its very nature, be closed to any wider public –
there can be no general access,
except via film, literature, and by leap of imagination.
It reminds me of the hidden artwork in medieval cathedrals,
at the tops of pillars and in the vaulting,
which only now can be appreciated through photography,
created by sculptors and painters to the greater glory of God.
In Antarctica one is unaccustomedly hypersensitive to the act of
Creation itself as never before,
and of the fact that this continues,
and that it affects us,
and that we affect it.
Elsewhere on Earth,
man is the most successful mammal:
here he has only a precarious toe-hold,
his presence is minimal when compared to the many millions of
perfectly adapted seals.
It is a terrible, hostile wonderland,
where we can only just survive with the help of cocoons of alien clothes,
tents, heated huts, ships, aeroplanes.
And even then it's dicey.

Antarctic Symphony (Symphony No. 8)

Notes from a Cold Climate

Antarctic Symphony (Symphony No. 8)

Notes from a Cold Climate

Antarctic Symphony (Symphony No. 8)

Notes from a Cold Climate

Antarctic Symphony (Symphony No. 8)

Notes from a Cold Climate

Antarctic Symphony (Symphony No. 8)

Notes from a Cold Climate

Antarctic Symphony (Symphony No. 8)

Notes from a Cold Climate

Antarctic Symphony (Symphony No. 8)

Notes from a Cold Climate

Antarctic Symphony (Symphony No. 8)

Notes from a Cold Climate

Antarctic Symphony (Symphony No. 8)

Notes from a Cold Climate

Antarctic Symphony (Symphony No. 8)

Notes from a Cold Climate

Antarctic Symphony (Symphony No. 8)

Notes from a Cold Climate

Antarctic Symphony (Symphony No. 8)

ONE OF THE MOST SERENDIPITOUS MOMENTS CAME WHEN A SNOW AVALANCHE POURED AND BILLOWED DOWN THE MOUNTAIN DIRECTLY TO STARBOARD –

IMAGINE THE MIGHTIEST, GENTLEST, LONGEST WHISPER EVER – WE WERE ENVELOPED IN MAD, DANCING FLAKES, A WHITE-OUT

Antarctic Symphony (Symphony No. 8)

Notes from a Cold Climate

Antarctic Symphony (Symphony No. 8)

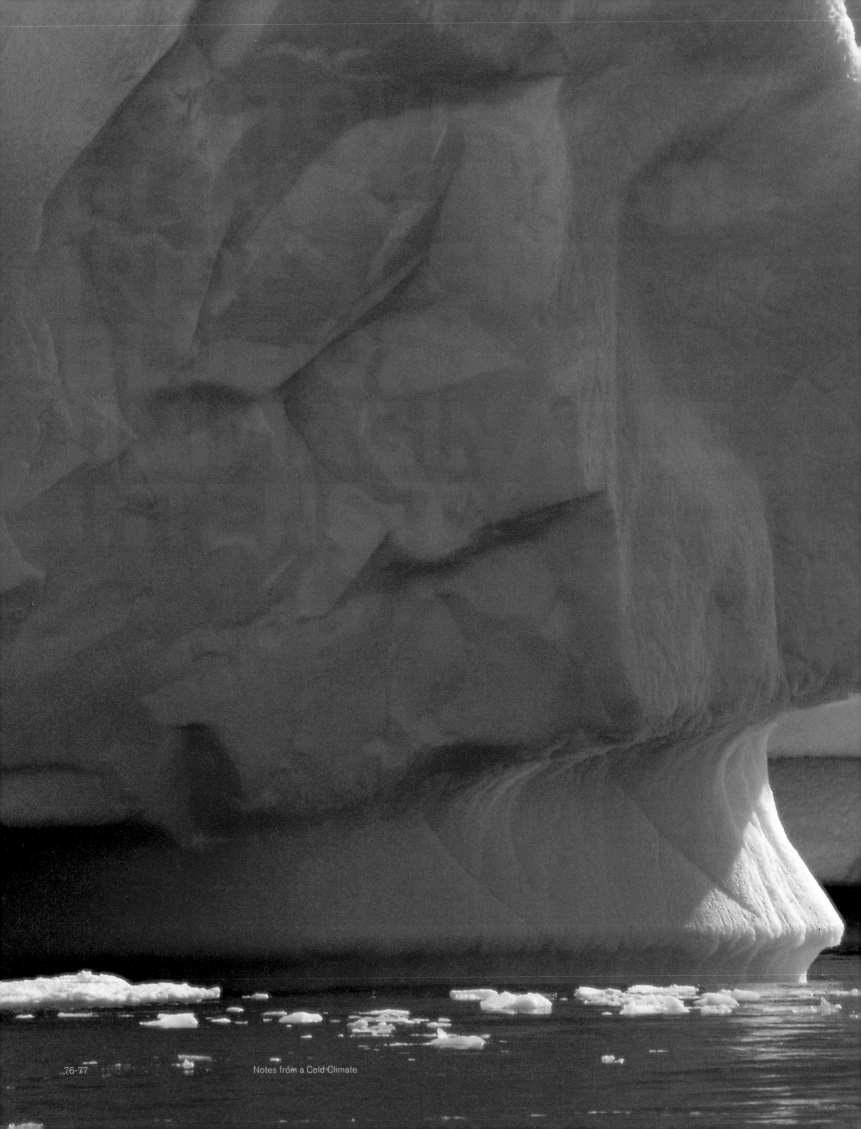

Notes from a Cold Climate

Antarctic Symphony (Symphony No. 8)

Notes from a Cold Climate

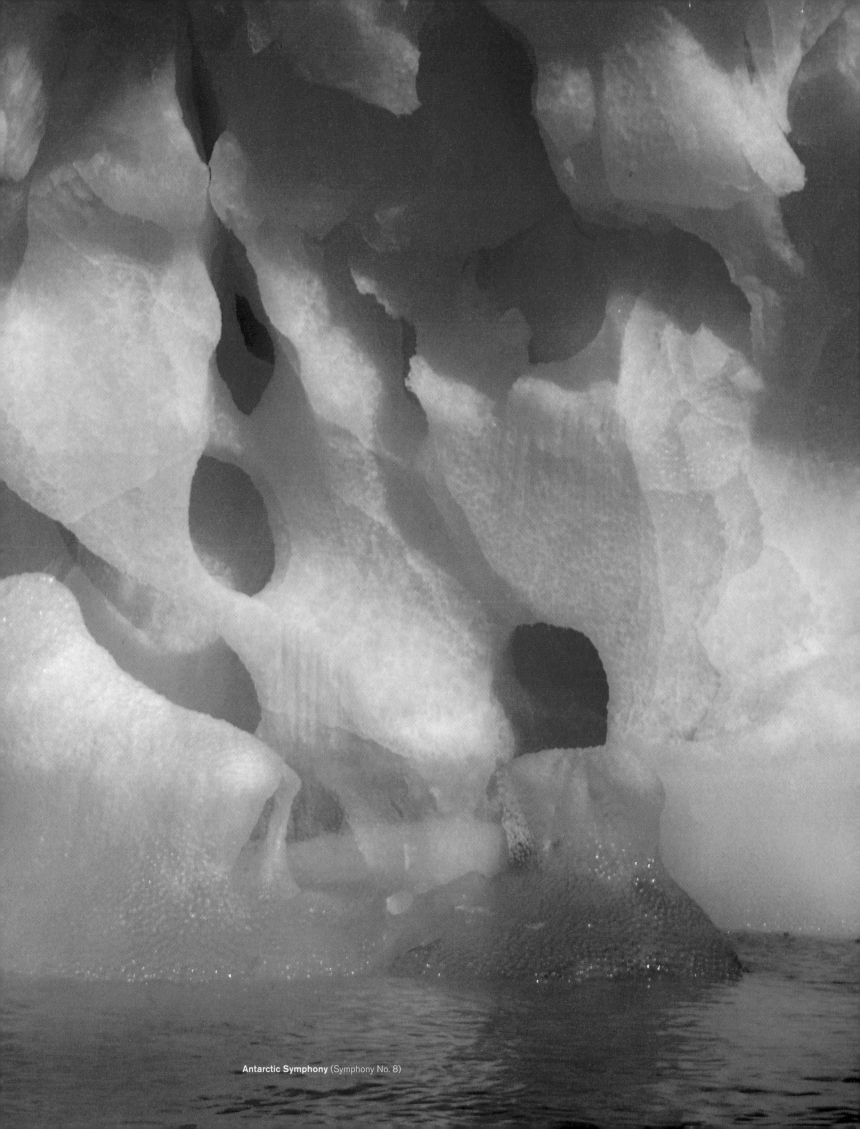

Antarctic Symphony (Symphony No. 8)

Notes from a Cold Climate

Antarctic Symphony (Symphony No. 8)

EVEN THE UNFROZEN SEA-WATER WAS LIKE OIL, THICKLY VISCOUS

Antarctic Symphony (Symphony No. 8)

Notes from a Cold Climate

Antarctic Symphony (Symphony No. 8)

Notes from a Cold Climate

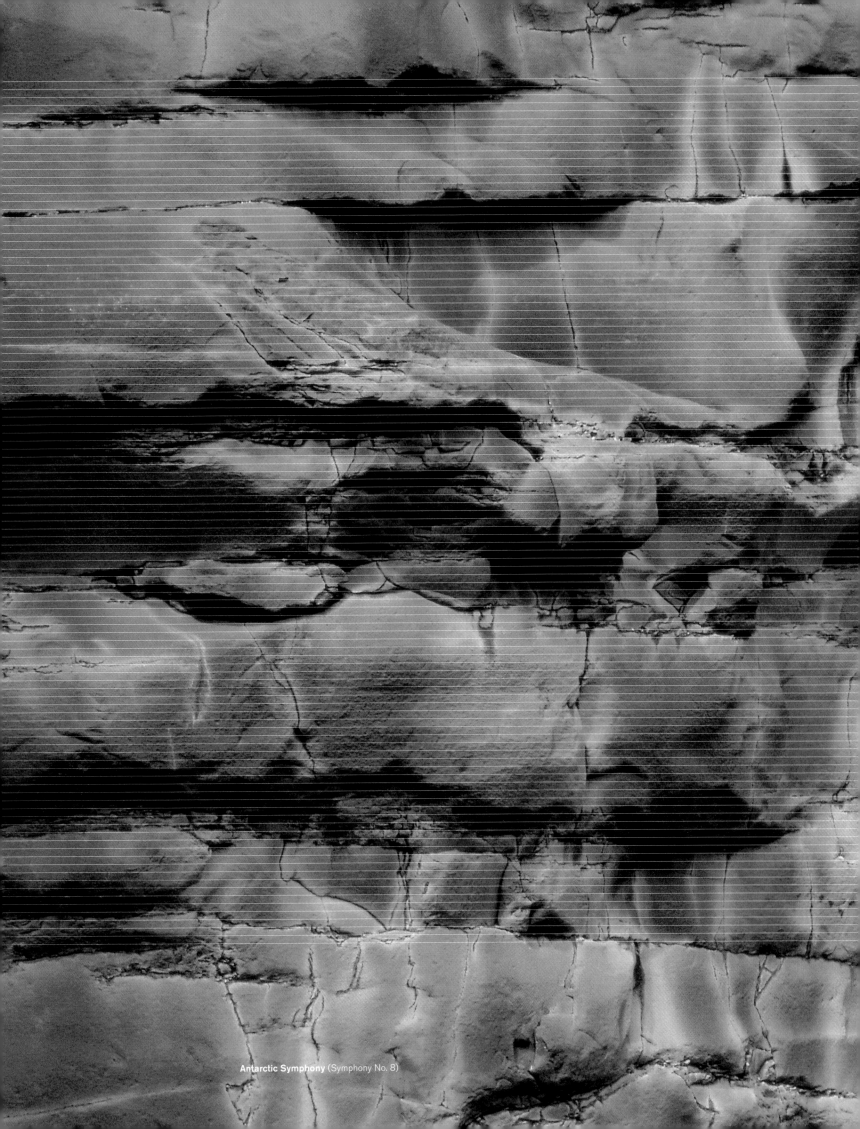

Antarctic Symphony (Symphony No. 8)

Notes from a Cold Climate

Antarctic Symphony (Symphony No. 8)

Notes from a Cold Climate

Antarctic Symphony (Symphony No. 8)

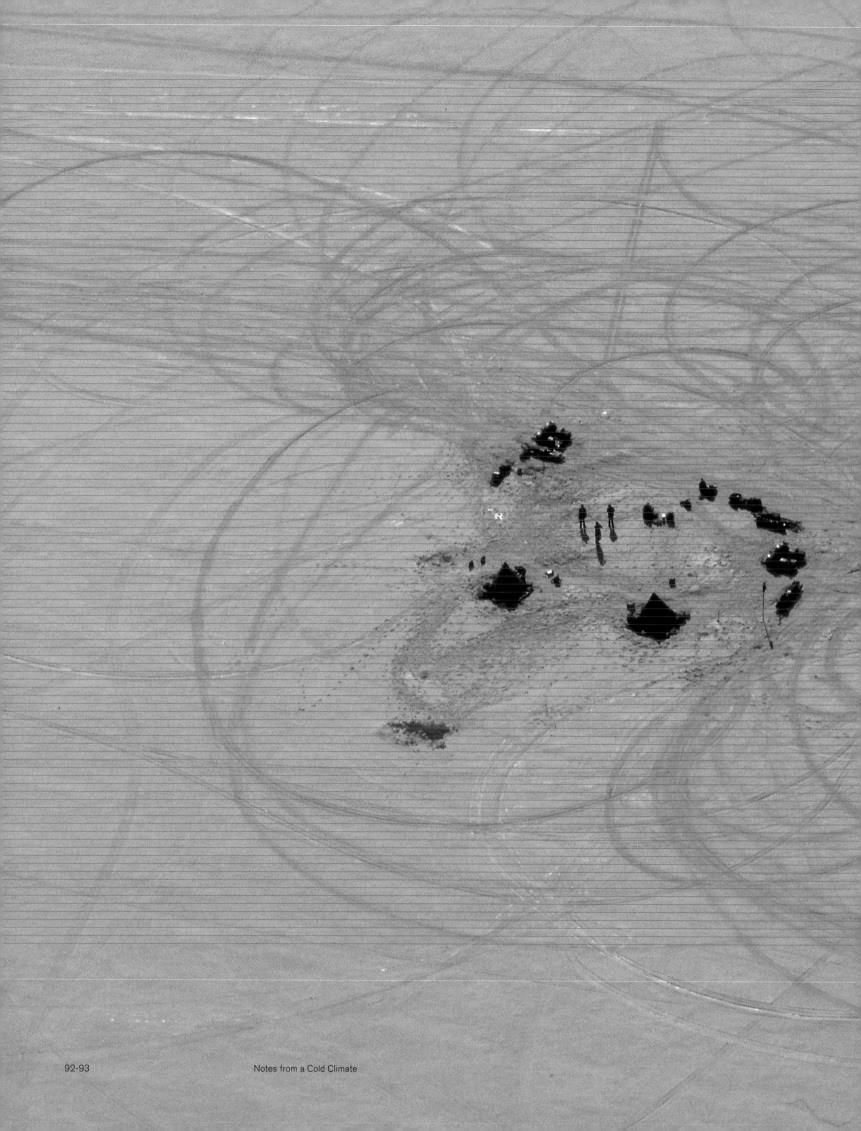

Notes from a Cold Climate

Antarctic Symphony (Symphony No. 8)

Notes from a Cold Climate

Antarctic Symphony (Symphony No. 8)

Notes from a Cold Climate

Antarctic Symphony (Symphony No. 8)

Notes from a Cold Climate

Antarctic Symphony (Symphony No. 8)

Notes from a Cold Climate

Antarctic Symphony (Symphony No. 8)

Antarctic Symphony (Symphony No. 8)

Notes from a Cold Climate

Antarctic Symphony (Symphony No. 8)

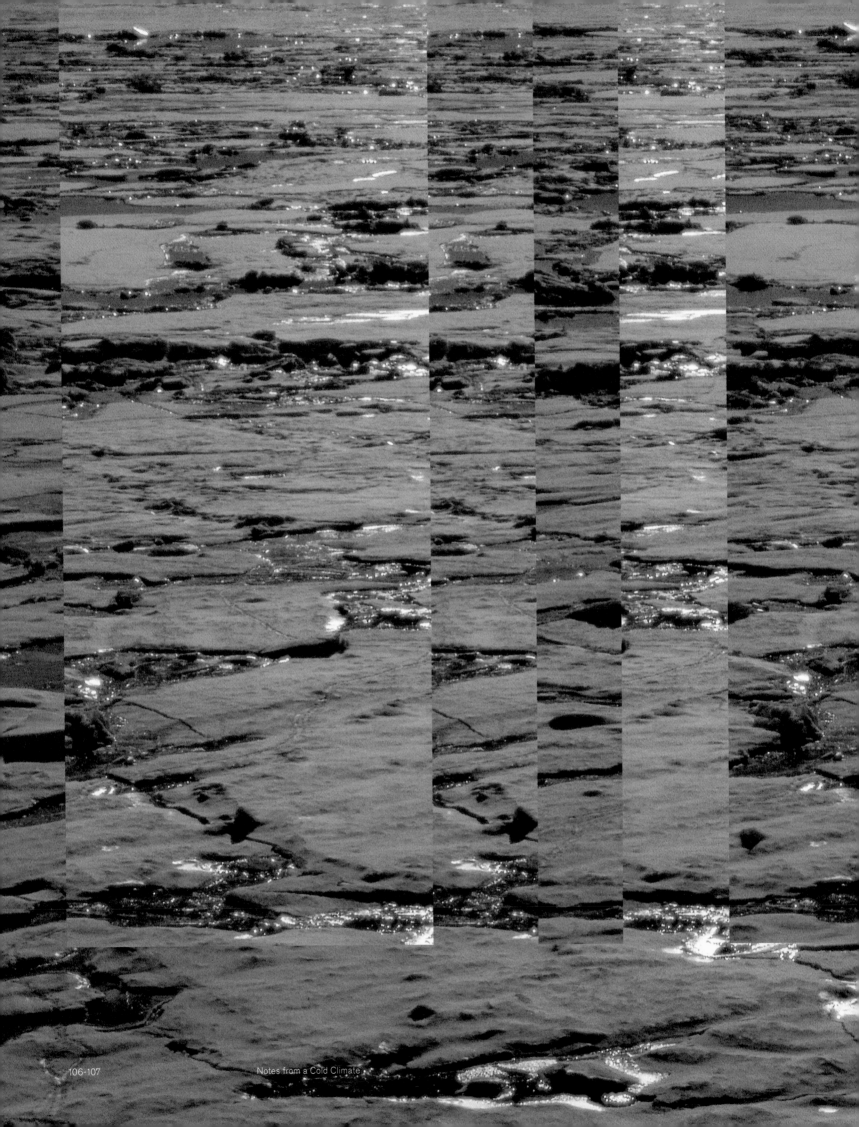

Notes from a Cold Climate

Antarctic (Symphony No. 8)

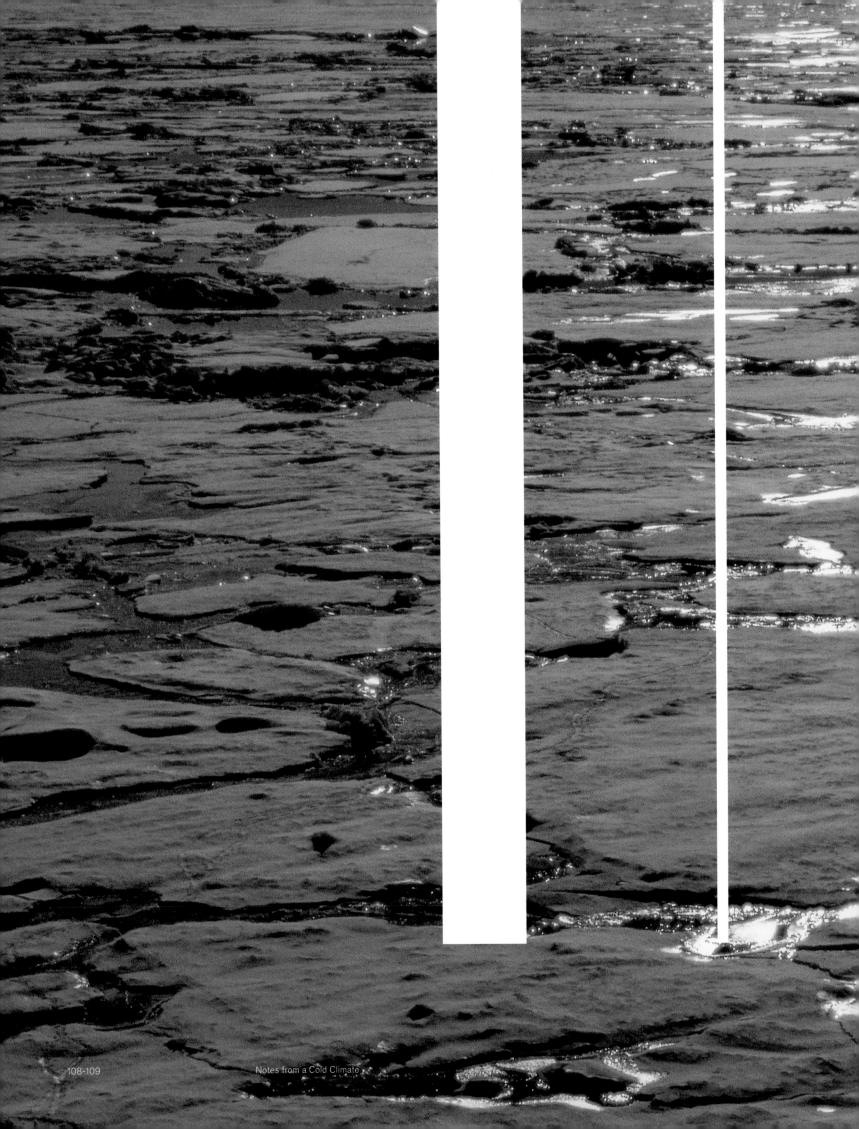

Notes from a Cold Climate

Antarctic Symphony (Symphony No. 8)

Notes from a Cold Climate

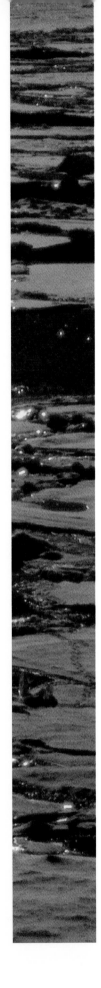

Antarctic Symphony (Symphony No. 8)

Antarctic Symphony (Symphony No. 8)

Notes from a Cold Climate

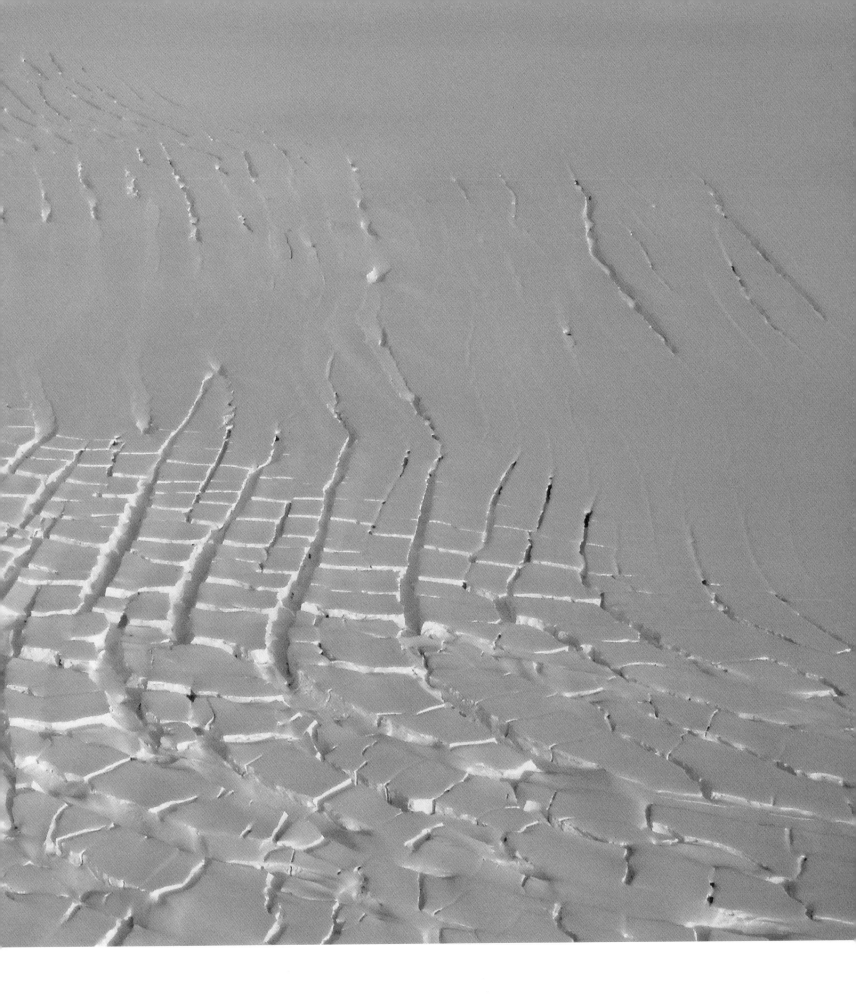

Antarctic Symphony (Symphony No. 8)

Notes from a Cold Climate

Antarctic Symphony (Symphony No. 8)

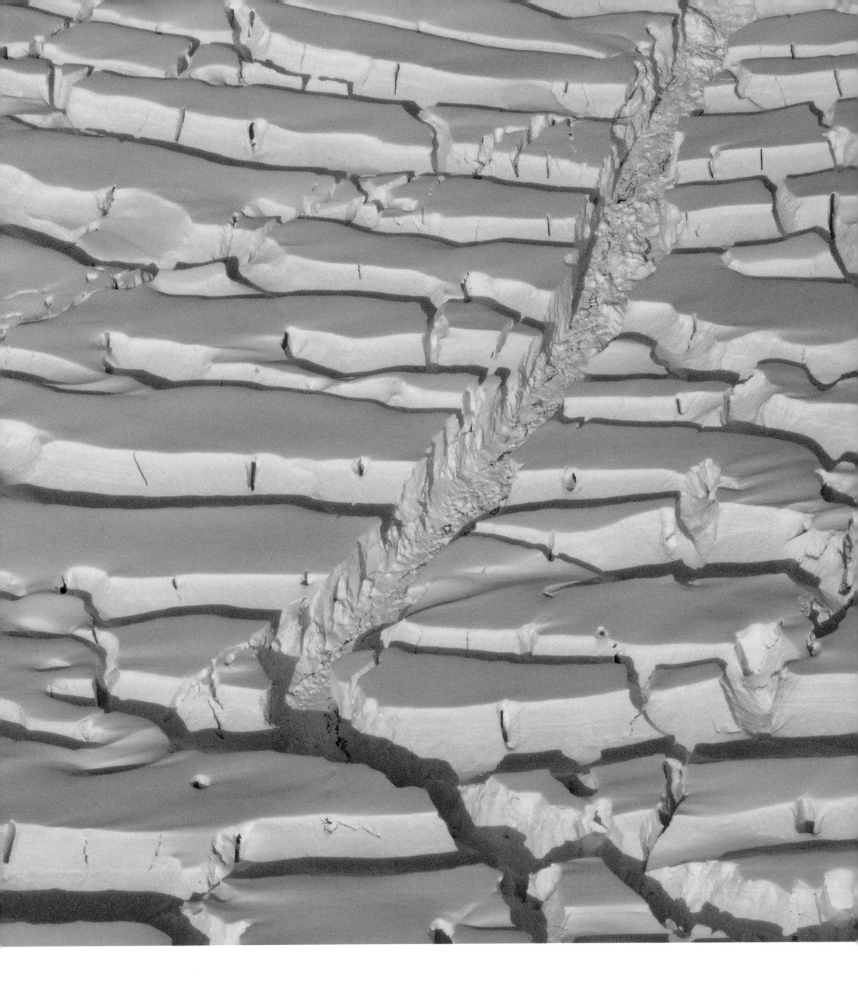

Notes from a Cold Climate

Antarctic Symphony (Symphony No. 8)

Notes from a Cold Climate

Antarctic Symphony (Symphony No. 8)

Antarctic Symphony (Symphony No. 8)

Notes from a Cold Climate

about earth tremors over a period of time, which ennables her to calculate new information about thicknesses of the earth's crust.

The plateau upon which we stand is ringed with peaks — so dramatic they have a hallucinatory quality, their sharp and intense integrated geometry having something of the surreal, or unreal aspect of those computer-generated landscapes you see in space movies. One peak is blackly strident under a perfectly sculpted half-sphere of snow-covered ice — you just cannot work out if there is a hollow under the ice, reaching back to the mountaintop, or if the mountaintop bulges out from beneath the ice : it is alarming to see the ice and the mountain move in their spaces, as the eye interprets and re-interprets the visible evidence.

Andy looks concerned, as the wind freshens, and lashes the snow up around the plane's skis — but eventually, before it becomes critical, two black dots split the junction of dizzy white and powder blue, slowly becoming toiling red figures, and at last we learn of the success of Anya's findings. On the return to Rothera, we make trial landings on ice, with a view to establishing a place to deposit barrels, to refuel twin otters on flights

Notes from a Cold Climate

Antarctic Symphony (Symphony No. 8)

Notes from a Cold Climate

Antarctic Symphony (Symphony No. 8)

Notes from a Cold Climate

Antarctic Symphony (Symphony No. 8)

Notes from a Cold Climate

Antarctic Symphony (Symphony No. 8)

Antarctic Symphony (Symphony No. 8)

Notes from a Cold Climate

Antarctic Symphony (Symphony No. 8)

Notes from a Cold Climate

Antarctic Symphony (Symphony No. 8)

Notes from a Cold Climate

Antarctic Symphony (Symphony No. 8)

Britain in the Antarctic

British Antarctic Survey (BAS) is responsible for the majority of the UK's research activity in Antarctica. Of the 27 nations involved in Antarctic research, Britain has the longest, and possibly the most distinguished, record of exploration. Captain James Cook first circumnavigated the continent from 1773-75 and claimed the subantarctic island of South Georgia for Britain. Having endured for months the violent storms, grey mists, and freezing conditions of the Southern Ocean without once sighting the continent, Cook may be forgiven for his view that, *"Should anyone possess the resolution and fortitude to elucidate this point by pushing yet further south than I have done, I shall not envy him the fame of his discovery, but I make bold to declare that the world will derive no benefit from it".*

However, Captain Cook could not have guessed that Antarctica would play such a key role in the world's climate system and in controlling global mean sea level, nor that through the formation of the 'ozone hole' it would provide such a sensitive litmus of mankind's ability to pollute on a planetary scale. Antarctica may be remote and hostile, but its behaviour is relevant to us all.

Although initial Antarctic exploration focused on the commercial exploitation of seals, the first British scientific expeditions began in the 19th century with observations of the Earth's magnetic field, marine biology, oceanography and mapping. By the early 20th century Antarctica had entered the Heroic Age, with Scott and Shackleton becoming national icons.

A number of Antarctic expeditions took place between the world wars. Thirteen voyages during the Discovery Investigations (1925-39) made important advances in the biology of the oceans and provided information needed to improve the charts of Antarctic and subantarctic islands. John Rymill led the last British expedition before the Second World War to Graham Land in 1934-37. Over three years he carried out detailed scientific programmes on the Antarctic mainland, covering geology, meteorology, glaciology and biology.

During the Second World War, the British Government dispatched a secret admiralty operation, code-name Tabarin, to establish small bases on the Antarctic Peninsula for reconnaissance and meteorology. After the war the project was taken over by the Colonial Office and renamed the Falkland Islands Dependencies Survey (FIDS). This was the beginning of an enterprise that, although political and strategic in its origins, grew into the major international scientific organisation that is the British Antarctic Survey.

The last privately funded Antarctic expeditions were mounted by Duncan Carse between 1951-57, and surveyed the whole of South Georgia, producing the first accurate maps of the island.

Since that time almost all British scientific and survey work in Antarctica has been funded by the Government and organised by FIDS and then BAS. In 1967, BAS became a component of the Natural Environment Research Council.

Operating in the Earth's most hostile environment

Early Antarctic history is full of heroic failure and battles against the elements. Conducting world-class science in the region presents challenges not normally encountered by researchers working elsewhere in the world.

Scientific programmes, and the logistics to support five research stations, are planned and executed from the BAS UK headquarters in Cambridge where there are specialised laboratories, cold rooms, an aquarium, a mapping and data centre, administrative offices, workshops and stores.

Rothera research station, off the Antarctic Peninsula, accommodates up to 120 people during the austral summer. Most of BAS's geological and glaciological field research is co-ordinated from here and the Bonner Laboratory boasts excellent facilities for biologists studying animal and plant life in the surrounding seas and islands.

Halley research station on the Brunt Ice Shelf is the UK's most southerly Antarctic station and specialises in studies of the Earth's atmosphere from ground level to its outer limits. The polar regions are unique 'windows on space' that allow studies of the impact of the sun's activity on the Earth's magnetic field and 'space weather'.

The subantarctic island of South Georgia has two research stations. The island, once a centre of the whaling industry, is internationally important for its native wildlife populations, marine life and valuable fish stocks.

Bird Island research station at the north-west tip of the island is the centre for studies on the Southern Ocean ecosystem. This work plays a key role in providing advice to international bodies on the conservation of marine living resources. During the austral summer around six researchers study population dynamics of birds and seals and their interaction with valuable marine resources.

King Edward Point research station is an applied fisheries laboratory devoted to providing scientific advice on managing a sustainable commercial fishery around the island. Around six scientists work there in the austral summer.

Signy research station on the South Orkney Islands operates during the austral summer only supporting eight to ten scientists studying terrestrial and freshwater biology. Throughout the year an automatic camera records sea ice conditions to maintain the 50-year record obtained when the station was continuously occupied.

To support its research programmes BAS operates two ships, four Twin Otter aircraft (fitted with wheels and skis) and one Dash-7 aircraft that also provides the intercontinental airlink from Rothera to the Falkland Islands.

The ice-strengthened Royal Research Ship *James Clark Ross* is one of the most advanced and capable oceanographic research vessels afloat. The second Royal Research Ship *Ernest Shackleton's* principal role is the resupply of stations, although it can support limited scientific investigations also. In addition, BAS receives valuable support from the Royal Navy's *HMS Endurance,* whose helicopters often carry scientists and equipment to areas inaccessible by BAS ships or aircraft.

International and UK collaboration

Antarctica's international position, strengthened by the Antarctic Treaty (ratified in 1961), is a remarkable example of what may be achieved by co-operation between nations despite political and cultural differences. BAS works closely with the UK Foreign and Commonwealth Office to sustain an active and influential presence and leadership role in Antarctic affairs.

The Antarctic Treaty encourages member nations to work together on joint scientific programmes. The amount of collaboration varies widely and depends on both the scientific requirement of a programme and the resources that each country is willing to deploy. BAS has active links with scientists from all over the world. International Antarctic research programmes, in which BAS participates, are devised through the Scientific Committee on Antarctic Research.

Antarctic science: the challenges of global change

Antarctica plays a crucial role in understanding global change – past, present and future.

Processes taking place there affect the world's climate and its oceans. Preserved in its massive ice sheet is a record of climate for the last 500,000 years, from which emerges the natural rhythm of global change and humanity's recent intervention, and the link to the atmospheric concentrations of greenhouse gases. The stability of the Antarctic ice sheet is directly connected to a change in world sea level. The sustained retreat of several ice shelves has reinforced the need for computer models to assess the effects of possible future climate warming on the ice sheet. In the spring, ozone is destroyed above Antarctica, and more ultra-violet radiation reaches the Earth's surface over an area that extends beyond the Antarctic continent.

Southern Ocean ecosystem

The Southern Ocean connects the Atlantic, Indian and Pacific oceans. Although cold and often ice-covered it is biologically extremely rich. The Southern Ocean has often suffered from over-fishing, sometimes bringing species such as the great whales close to extinction. To avoid future long-term damage, scientific data are required for the management of the globally significant fisheries for fin fish, squid and krill (a shrimp-like organism eaten by whales, birds and seals). Unlike other world fisheries, Antarctic catches are regulated to preserve the entire ecosystem, not just the commercially important species.

Life at the edge

Less than 1 per cent of the Antarctic continent is free of ice and snow. In this hostile environment, ecologically simple communities of plants and other organisms have evolved with the capacity to survive prolonged freezing and desiccation. By contrast, the marine coastal environment of the Antarctic is probably the most thermally stable environment at the surface of the Earth. Seawater temperatures are low year-round, while ice cover and plankton blooms are seasonal. The biological communities are rich and diverse and have adapted to live within a narrow temperature range. Comparing the way in which species cope with these two distinct environments will lead to new understanding of how species cope with environmental change.

The Earth's outer atmosphere
Out at the edges of our atmosphere, charged particles accelerated in the outer atmosphere of the sun produce the stunning auroral displays seen in polar regions. From time to time these magnetic storms cause serious damage on Earth. Satellites can be disabled, terrestrial radio communications disrupted, and power transmission systems damaged, causing electricity blackouts. An early detection of these storms and a prediction of their possible damage has great technical and commercial importance.

Antarctica, lying close to the magnetic pole, is uniquely sited to measure the 'weather' in the upper atmosphere, using radars, cameras and other instruments. The challenge is to understand the physics of the processes involved in energy transfer in the upper atmosphere, so that a predictive model of weather in this region becomes possible.

Geographical evolution
For much of geographical time, Antarctica formed the centre of a large land-mass called Gondwana, which also included South America, Africa, India, Australia and New Zealand. It fragmented into separate pieces over a period of 160 million years and moved apart from the continents we know today. Geologists are uncertain as to why very large continents like Gondwana disintegrate but the break-up processes appear to involve 'hot spots' that originate in the Earth's mantle. Antarctic rocks still have much to reveal about the mechanisms surrounding the break-up and the tectonic forces involved. This pursuit is fundamental to understanding environmental change and the evolution of life over geological time, and can be applied on a wider scale to the geology of other continents.

Conservation and management
A growing political awareness of the fragility of the Antarctic led to The Protocol on Environmental Protection to the Antarctic Treaty (1991), adopted into UK legislation by the Antarctic Act (1994). The protocol provides for the comprehensive protection of the region and designates the Antarctic 'a natural reserve devoted to peace and science'. The protocol stresses

the need for environmental monitoring and scientific research in the fields of environmental impact assessment, waste disposal, the prevention of marine pollution, area protection and management, and the conservation of Antarctic flora and fauna.

BAS, in common with other Antarctic research organisations, operates a stringent environmental management policy to ensure UK compliance and undertakes relevant research.

The photographs
The photographs featured in this book were taken by Pete Bucktrout during Sir Peter Maxwell Davies' inspirational visit to Antarctica.

There is a tradition of photographing Antarctica reaching back to the Heroic Age, with Ponting (Scott's official photographer) and Hurley (who travelled with Shackleton). Pete Bucktrout is one of two professional photographers employed by BAS to record its work for scientific purposes and public awareness. In addition to supporting BAS science his photography has appeared in many books, magazines and newspapers in the UK and overseas. Images from his trip with Sir Peter Maxwell Davies were exhibited at the Royal College of Music in 2000 as part of the Creating Sparks Science Festival. During his 11 years with BAS, Pete Bucktrout has travelled to Antarctica five times.

Philharmonia Orchestra
Founded by Walter Legge in 1945, the Philharmonia Orchestra is acknowledged as one of the world's great orchestras. The distinguished maestro Christoph von Dohnanyi has been the Philharmonia's Principal Conductor since 1997, and under his leadership the orchestra has consolidated its central position in British music life. As well as its position as Resident Orchestra at the Royal Festival Hall in London, the Philharmonia has developed successful regional residencies at Bedford Corn Exchange, De Montfort Hall in Leicester and The Anvil in Basingstoke, which have provided an ideal opportunity to expand the Philharmonia's dynamic programme of education and community work.

The world's most recorded symphony orchestra, the Philharmonia has won several major awards during the past few seasons, and has received unanimous critical acclaim for its innovative programming policy and its commitment to performing

and commissioning new music. The Philharmonia is also one of the UK's most energetic musical ambassadors, with residencies at the Chatelet Theatre in Paris and the Megaron in Athens, as well as undertaking a busy schedule of appearances in major concert halls worldwide.

Sir Peter Maxwell Davies
by John Warnaby
Composers generally fall into two broad categories: those who pioneer new compositional ideas, including playing techniques, and who are often regarded as iconoclastic because they appear to reject tradition; and those who use a process of synthesis to sum up recent developments. Sir Peter Maxwell Davies has fulfilled both roles, sometimes in the same work.

He was born on 8 September 1934 in Salford, now part of Greater Manchester. His first important musical experience occurred when he was four, when he was taken to a local production of Gilbert and Sullivan's *The Gondoliers.* Shortly afterwards, he began receiving piano lessons. His parents actively encouraged him, and soon he gravitated naturally to composing. His first public performance took place in 1942, when a piano piece was played in the BBC Home Service's *Children's Hour.* A great deal of juvenilia followed, and he now suggests that some of the pieces he produced in his teens already contain 'fingerprints' of his mature style.

However, music was discouraged at Leigh Grammar School, so Max continued this aspect of his education independently. He was helped by the Henry Watson Library in Manchester, where he could study a vast range of scores, and by the advent of the BBC *Third Programme,* which introduced him to a great deal of unfamiliar music and enabled him to broaden his cultural and scientific interests. He memorised many works from the standard symphonic repertoire but also concentrated on Renaissance polyphony, as well as Indian music. After obtaining his A-levels, he gained admission to both the Royal Manchester College of Music and Manchester University.

His university course ultimately led to a Master of Arts degree, which he obtained for a dissertation on the rhythmic organisation of Indian ragas; but his studies at the Royal Manchester College were far less conventional. The composition teaching took little account of 20th century music, but Max

found common cause with a group of like-minded students which included Alexander Goehr, Harrison Birtwistle, Elgar Howarth and John Ogdon. They received sympathetic support from Richard Hall, the only tutor with any real knowledge of contemporary composition, and formed an ensemble called New Music Manchester, which led to them being dubbed 'The Manchester School'. Their repertoire included their own compositions, together with a variety of scores by contemporary European composers, which Goehr was able to acquire with the help of his father, the conductor Walter Goehr. They presented at least one concert in London.

While at the college, Max submitted a brief, single-movement string quartet to the Society for the Promotion of New Music, which was rejected as unplayable, and then wrote his Trumpet Sonata for Elgar Howarth and either himself or John Ogdon to perform. He described it as *Opus No. 1,* and followed it with his Five Piano Pieces, *Op. 2,* after which he dispensed with opus numbers entirely. His catalogue now contains nearly 300 works in all genres, and is growing rapidly. Besides more than 60 orchestral scores, several stage works, choral, chamber and incidental music, there is a large body of educational material, designed for children of different ages, as well as many occasional pieces which Max has often written at great speed.

Max's involvement with music education stems largely from personal experience, and led him to become Head of Music at Cirencester Grammar School from 1959-1962. While there, he pioneered many ideas, particularly as regards practical music-making, and extended these activities to include children who could not read music. Besides forming the basis of his subsequent educational activities, these ideas have become standard practice, especially in recent years. Before Cirencester, however, Max obtained an Italian Government Scholarship, enabling him to study with the Italian composer Goffredo Petrassi in Rome, in 1957-58. Petrassi introduced a degree of rigour which Max had not previously experienced, and this was a crucial factor in the completion of his first major orchestral score, entitled *Prolation.*

The title refers to one of the fundamental principles of medieval and renaissance polyphony which Max used in conjunction with serial methods in many of his early works. *Prolation* thus became a key work in his early development, not only winning the Olivetti Composition Prize, but also representing Britain at the 1959 festival organised by the International Society for Contemporary Music.

Max had established the fundamentals of his creative technique in the *Sonata for Trumpet* and *Five Pieces for Piano*. The strong sense of continuity in his output has its origins in the way he applied variants of the serial method to the formation of a pre-compositional grid, or 'transposition square', which would contain the basic material of the work, and the means by which it would be transformed. From an early stage, he employed fragments of plainsong as source material, and these could have symbolic, as well as strictly musical significance. An early example was *Alma Redemptoris Mater,* for instrumental sextet.

Initially, these transformation processes were restricted to pitch, but soon they were extended to rhythm, and even to the overall architecture of the composition. The principle is analogous to that of upgrading a computer program, and has been applied with increasing refinement throughout his career. Accordingly, serialism was replaced by pitch 'sets' of varying length; then, transposition squares were used to generate hierarchical structures in which the basic scheme was applied to several levels of organisation.

By the time he wrote *Prolation,* Max had established a formidable repertoire of compositional strategies. They helped him enhance his considerable facility as a composer, and the flexibility of his style, but did not influence the character of individual scores.

A curious feature of Max's biography has been the importance of the final year of each decade. Thus, in 1959, together with *Prolation,* the *St. Michael Sonata* for 17 wind instruments – premiered at the Cheltenham Festival – formed the culmination of the first phase of his career. The programme note revealed a broad view of music history, together with the fact that symbolic features were as important as technical considerations. The libretto of his first opera, *Taverner,* was taking shape, based on what was then known about the life of the Tudor composer, while his arrangement of sections of the *Monteverdi Vespers* for performance at Cirencester led to the development

of an alternative tonal repertoire, exemplified by the choral and instrumental sequence, *O Magnum Mysterium.* Soon, however, the distinction between his educational and concert music became less pronounced, as he drew on elements of the *Sonata Sopra Sancta Maria,* from the *Vespers,* for three works written in the early 1960s. These were the *String Quartet,* the *Leopardi Fragments,* for soprano, contralto, and ensemble, and the *Sinfonia,* for chamber orchestra. They exhibited a tendency to generate clusters of works from a single source, or compositional idea; their range of expression was broader than hitherto, and this had a bearing on the creation of largescale structures.

However, the major structural breakthrough was achieved with the two *Fantasias* on an 'In Nomine' of John Taverner. The original 'In Nomine' from Taverner's *Missa Gloria Tibi Trinitas* formed the basis of countless keyboard pieces by several generations of renaissance and baroque British composers, and in his *Seven In Nomine* for ensemble, Max interspersed some of these with his own contrapuntal elaborations.

The two *Fantasias* were conceived on an entirely different scale, especially the second, which was a work of symphonic proportions. It was substantially based on material from the first act of the opera, and was written while Max was a post-graduate student at Princeton University. He had won a Harkness Fellowship, enabling him to study with Roger Sessions and Earl Kim in the Music Faculty, where he also encountered Milton Babbitt, and a fellow student, Stephen Pruslin, who became one of Max's main collaborators for more than 20 years. In addition, there was a good deal of contact between the arts and sciences, so that it was possible to learn something about the latest research in such fields as particle physics, etc. It was also difficult to avoid the impact of rampant commercialism on American society, a factor which ultimately led to the opera, *Resurrection,* when a similar economic philosophy was introduced to Britain in the 1980s.

Max has always been preoccupied with the role of the artist in society, and after his sojourn in the United States, and a year's teaching at the University of South Australia, he returned to Britain in the late 1960s at a time of radical social and cultural change. His style was undergoing an equally radical transformation, in response to the

turbulence associated with the composition of *Taverner.* The Mahlerian intensity of the *Second Taverner Fantasia* had been superseded by the violent expressionism of *Revelation and Fall,* for soprano and 16 instrumentalists, where the singer appears at a lectern, dressed in a vivid red nun's habit, and sometimes has to scream through a loudhailer. Parallels were implied between John Taverner and Trakl, in that both men were outsiders searching for religious, or artistic truth. They were extended by suggesting a link between the destructive aspects of religious ideology in the 16th century, and the dogmatic pursuit of integral serialism developed by composers in the 1950s.

There was also a conflict between Max's theological interests and the continuing intolerance of religious authorities towards the social changes of the time. By making explicit the implications of Schoenberg's early atonal scores, Max was able to respond to the lurid imagery of Trakl's verse, and by alluding to the popular music of Trakl's era, a further parallel was forged between the decadent final years of the Austro-Hungarian Empire, and the cultural fragmentation of the 1960s. Similar procedures were employed in *Missa Super L'Homme Armé,* for reciter and ensemble, where techniques influenced by James Joyce's *Ulysses* were applied to material derived from an incomplete 15th century setting of the Mass; *Eight Songs for a Mad King,* again, for voice and ensemble, combined monologues spoken by the supposedly insane King George III with fragments of Handel's *Messiah;* and *Vesalii Icones,* for dancer, solo cello and ensemble, was based on the *Stations of the Cross,* but interpreted in terms of a sequence of anatomical drawings by Andreas Vesalius.

All these works were satellites of *Taverner,* where a link was established between the growing significance of symbolism and the development of 'transformation processes', involving the systematic alteration of sets of pitch, or interval classes, thereby turning a theme into its inversion, or transforming a fragment of one plainsong into another. Thus, the symbolism of the so-called 'death chord' – D, E, F sharp, G sharp – was extended to the Taverner-related scores, and the theatrical elements enhanced their popularity. They secured Max's reputation as a leading exponent of music-theatre, and the conjunction of parody with

controversial subjects, including elements of hysteria, or madness, gave concerts by the Pierrot Players – later renamed Fires of London – a provocative character. Madness, in various manifestations, has remained a central theme in Max's output and is usually associated with some form of rejection of authority, frequently represented by a King figure. The mocking presence of a jester also symbolises the element of self-destruction this entails. The music for Ken Russell's film *The Devils, Miss Donnithorne's Maggot,* or the ballet, *Caroline Mathilde* are typical examples, but the peak of the expressionist phase had already been reached in *Vesalii Icones,* culminating with a mock resurrection, accompanied by a foxtrot.

Foxtrots were equated with bad taste, as well as falsity, and were particularly prominent in *St. Thomas Wake,* foxtrot for orchestra, where they reflected Max's recollections of wartime broadcasts in which news bulletins were interspersed with 1930s dance music. The foxtrots were allocated to a typical nine-piece band, but the violence of the orchestral transformations indicated that the level of psychological tension could no longer be sustained without threatening to undermine the composer's creative personality. Indeed, throughout this period, he had been writing *Worldes Blis* in an attempt to 'reintegrate the scattered fragments' of his personality, and it remains his largest single orchestral movement to date. It also constituted a vital stage in the development of Davies the symphonist.

However, the vital ingredient proved to be the discovery of Orkney, and particularly the work of George Mackay Brown, whose poetry, fiction, and journalism introduced Max to the local community, together with the history and folklore of the islands. After the fallow year of 1970, this was virtually a new beginning, comprising not only Orkney-inspired scores, but pieces which looked back to the 1960s. Max's first Mackay Brown setting was *From Stone to Thorne,* written only two years after *Vesalii Icones,* and again evoking the *Stations of the Cross,* but this time in terms of the annual cycle of ploughing and harvesting. *Hymn to St. Magnus,* for soprano and ensemble, and *Stone Litany,* for mezzo-soprano and orchestra, quickly followed: both inspired by Mackay Brown, but setting, respectively, a medieval hymn to the Patron Saint of Orkney, and runic inscriptions carved in the burial chamber of Maeshowe.

Even in his earliest Orkney works, Max discovered a compositional equivalent of Mackay Brown's style and identified with two of the author's archetypal characters: the historical Earl Magnus Erlendson, and the mythological Storm Kolson, also known as The Blind Fiddler. They were associated with the ritual aspects of Orkney life, especially Mackay Brown's portrayal of the medieval era, when religious observance and folklore were integral features of daily experience. The former became the subject of the chamber opera, *The Martyrdom of St. Magnus,* based on the novel, *Magnus,* while the latter was celebrated in *The Blind Fiddler,* the largescale culmination of a sequence of song-cycles and, essentially, the counterpart of the chamber opera.

The 1970s were a particularly fruitful period for Max, as Orcadian influences were combined with elements of his earlier style. Some of the religious symbolism and the political aspects of *Taverner* were adapted to *The Martyrdom of St. Magnus,* but continuity was most clearly established at the technical level. *Worldes Blis* prefigured the slowly unfolding landscape Max soon discovered on Hoy, and some of its techniques were refined in *Hymn to St. Magnus.* The precise construction of the prehistoric tomb of Maeshowe not only inspired *Stone Litany,* but encouraged the evolution of Max's technique through the introduction of 'magic squares' as a means of controlling transformation processes over extended time-spans. *Ave Maris Stella* was the first major work to be based entirely on a magic square, and the choice was determined as much by symbolic, as technical considerations. The magic square of the moon, with its nine rows and columns, corresponded to the plainsong text praising Our Lady of the Sea, and in order to establish a symbolic link with the character of Blind Mary, who plays a crucial role in *The Martyrdom of St. Magnus,* a different version of the same square was used in the chamber opera. Accordingly, both works have nine distinct sections, but in the opera, pathways were devised which reflected the significance of the weaving motif in Mackay Brown's novel. As a consequence, his compositions became increasingly associated with a sense of place, and he began to achieve a recognisably consistent style.

By the mid 1970s, isorhythmic techniques from the medieval and early renaissance periods were being combined with elements of classical sonata-form, and sufficient flexibility, together with a wider range of expression, had been achieved to suggest even more ambitious projects.

Thus Max embarked on his cycle of symphonies, with a single-movement, provisionally entitled *Black Pentecost,* evolving into the four-movement structure of *Symphony No. 1.* This inaugurated a gradual change of emphasis from music-theatre, to orchestral music in general, and symphonies in particular. The first symphony was the culmination of a cluster of works, and subsequent symphonies have tended to follow a similar pattern. The difference was that the overall scheme of transformation processes for *Symphony No. 2* was devised, from the outset, as a clear four-movement structure. It emerged from an unusually wide range of scores completed during the late 1970s. These included adaptations of Mackay Brown texts to genres with which they had not previously been associated. *Westerlings,* for unaccompanied chorus, interspersed poetic evocations of the Vikings' discovery of Orkney with vocalised seascapes, while *Solstice of Light,* for solo tenor, chorus and organ, written for the recently formed St. Magnus Festival Chorus, set a specially written text in which environmental and other issues were incorporated into a brief outline of the Islands' history. Accordingly, *Solstice of Light* was linked to *The Two Fiddlers,* an opera for teenagers based on a Mackay Brown short story, and particularly *Black Pentecost,* a large orchestral work with mezzo and baritone soloists. The latter became the centrepiece of a successful protest by the local community against the prospect of uranium mining on Orkney, dramatising extracts from the final chapter of Mackay Brown's prophetic novel, *Greenvoe:* a fictional account of the destruction of a small island by a secret military organisation.

The events associated with the composition of *Black Pentecost* increased still further Max's identification with Orkney, which had led him to inaugurate the St. Magnus Festival, in 1977. Likewise, his remote croft, situated on one of the highest cliffs on the island of Hoy, probably encouraged him to fashion the libretto of his next chamber opera from a local legend about the mysterious disappearance of three lighthouse keepers. *The Lighthouse* is Max's most frequently performed stagework and encapsulates many of his most persistent themes; but *Symphony No. 2* is even more permeated with the sounds of the sea. Its formal plan was influenced by the observation of two distinct wave forms, which gave rise to alternating types of material. These provided elements of contrast in the individual movements. No less important was the symphony's luminous quality, inspired by the vivid reflection of sunlight in the bay beneath Max's study window. He responded with unusually consonant harmonies, combining modal and tonal elements, plus scintillating textures dominated by high pitched percussion. Yet the second symphony was the last work in which Max concentrated on such brilliant sonorities. In the early 1980s, he returned to the fundamentals of his musical personality, dispensing with features which he considered were becoming stylistic mannerisms. The process began with *Image, Reflection, Shadow,* for cimbalom and small ensemble, the *Brass Quintet,* and the *Piano and Organ Sonatas.* It reached its peak in the massive *Symphony No. 3,* which has been compared with Mahler's *Ninth Symphony.* Some commentators have also detected the influence of Schoenberg, but more specifically the symphony's formal outline, involving the presentation of the same material from different perspectives, was indebted to Brunelleschi's use of the *Fibonacci Series* in his church architecture.

The austerity of the third symphony was at least partly due to the reduction of the percussion section to only timpani, but it was also in keeping with the underlying mood of the 1980s. Another development which encouraged an economical approach to composition was the start of Max's fruitful association with the Scottish Chamber Orchestra (SCO). It began with the first performance of the song-cycle *Into the Labyrinth* at the 1983 St. Magnus Festival. Mackay Brown's text again dealt with environmental issues, but with a greater emphasis on renewal, which was curiously appropriate for Max, as his collaboration with the SCO enabled him to revive and extend the 'classical' aspect of his creative personality. The first performance of *Sinfonietta Accademica* soon followed, while the *Sinfonia Concertante,* for wind quintet, strings and timpani – originally written for the Academy of St. Martin-in-the-Fields – was added to complete a triptych.

Max became increasingly involved in the SCO's concerts, conducting Haydn, Mozart and early Beethoven, as well as his own music. In the manner of a typical court composer of the late 18th century, he then embarked on the Strathclyde Concerto Project, completing six solo concertos, two double concertos, a concerto grosso, featuring six soloists, and a concerto for orchestra in the space of nine years. The concertos were conceived in terms of dialogue rather than confrontation, but by the end of the cycle, every member of the orchestra had been required to display considerable virtuosity. The scheme also incorporated an important educational dimension involving the whole community and, as with the Fires of London, the SCO were encouraged to commission pieces from younger composers.

The Strathclyde Concertos reflected Max's other preoccupations, and even shared material with other compositions. These included further scores for the SCO written during and since the completion of the project. The most important was the fourth symphony, which summed up the harmonic language of its predecessors, based around the tritone B-F, and concentrating on intervals having a minor third-diminished seventh relationship. *Symphony No. 4* also compressed the traditional four movements into a continuous span, thereby combining the influences of Schoenberg and Sibelius; and scoring the work for chamber orchestra ensured the utmost economy of expression. The SCO have also been associated with some of Max's lighter music, as well as his recent involvement in works for chorus and orchestra. Accordingly, they participated in the premiere of *The Jacobite Rising,* while *Sea Elegy,* to texts by Mackay Brown, has been written for their 25th season.

Meanwhile, other factors encouraged altogether larger conceptions. Max relinquished the directorship of the St. Magnus Festival in 1986, and disbanded the Fires of London the following year. As part of a greater emphasis on orchestral music, long-term collaborations were established with various orchestras, particularly the BBC Philharmonic Orchestra, and the Royal Philharmonic Orchestra. It was therefore possible to appreciate the musical character of individual players, and to tailor their parts accordingly, as happened when writing for the Fires, or the SCO. Obviously, the degree of identification is much greater in the case of a concerto, and the challenge of writing for soloists was not restricted to the Strathclyde project. It began with the *Violin Concerto,* soon followed by the very different *Trumpet Concerto,* both composed during the second half of the 1980s. At the same time, he finally completed the opera, *Resurrection,* in response to the corrosive effects of the market economy on British society. Though, to some extent, the opera was originally conceived as a sequel to *Taverner,* it ultimately had more in common with popular culture. Hence, it developed ideas adumbrated in *The No.11 Bus.* Other ideas were adapted from Mackay Brown's short story, *The Two Fiddlers,* and the libretto suggested a work of immense satirical potential. However, the element of parody lacked the ferocity of the *Taverner*-related works, partly because the opera has still not had a completely satisfactory production, but possibly because Max's links with the relatively stable Orkney community distanced him from the worst excesses of greed and consumerism. Nevertheless, *Resurrection* appears to have encouraged a re-evaluation of earlier scores from the perspective of the 1990s. Besides the fact that Max's œuvre is unified by his expanding repertoire of transformation processes, structural, thematic, and even symbolic correspondences can be discerned between recent works and those of the late 1960s.

Even by Max's standards, the 1990s have been remarkably fruitful. In addition to the Strathclyde Concertos, the decade began with a sequence of music-theatre pieces for young children, commissioned by Longmans, followed by *The Turn of the Tide,* designed to enable children to integrate their own pieces into an orchestral score. There was also a second full-length ballet, *Caroline Mathilde,* from which two concert suites were extracted, whose structures shared certain affinities with *St. Thomas Wake* and *Worldes Blis,* respectively. A third ballet failed to materialise, becoming, instead, the purely orchestral choreographic poem, *The Beltane Fire.* This is a work of symphonic proportions, but its form is analogous to that of a Mackay Brown short story. There is a clear narrative thread, and each of the characters is 'sketched' in terms of different kinds of music. Above all, the work includes elements of Max's

popular style, played on instruments associated with folk music, and the attempt to integrate these into one of his most ambitious and profoundly Orcadian scores has been largely successful.

The fifth symphony was equally, if not more, successful, at least partly in view of its concision. As in *St. Thomas Wake,* or *Vesalii Icones,* it involved the constant interplay between three distinct layers of material, but without any suggestion of parody, or stylistic fragmentation. It is also the work in which the influence of Sibelius has been most evident. Sibelius' seventh symphony was the obvious model, but in Max's fifth, the allusions to a conventional four-movement scheme were superseded by the alternation between episodes of fast and slow music. Particularly impressive was the ability to create timeless passages in a work of such economy, so that even after repeated hearings, the fifth symphony seems much larger than its 25-minute duration.

Symphony No. 6 developed ideas from its predecessor – gradually allowing the background material to rise to the surface – but returned to the size and scope of the first three symphonies. However, more significant was the parallel between its three-movement structure, complete with extended slow finale, and that of the second Taverner Fantasia. Like the *Fantasia, Symphony No. 6* was also based on a pre-existing composition – the concert overture *Time and the Raven,* written for the 50th anniversary of the United Nations – thereby echoing the early renaissance practice of extending a motet into a parody mass.

Other orchestral works have followed, including the *Piccolo Concerto,* the *Piano Concerto,* with its many references to the history of the genre, and *A Reel of Seven Fishermen,* which can be regarded as a successor of *The Beltane Fire.* There have also been several shorter pieces, inspired by childhood recollections. The most important development, however, has been the Orkney Saga project, which will ultimately comprise 14 works, reflecting Max's responses to Mackay Brown's captions for a series of tapestries commemorating the role of Orkneymen in the Crusades and displayed in St. Magnus Cathedral, Kirkwall. The project will cover different genres, but the first two pieces are purely orchestral, apart from the introduction of a solo treble at the conclusion of *Orkney Saga II.* Both works last approximately

20 minutes, and in *Orkney Saga I,* the composer presents a fresh approach to the orchestra, with a formal originality and tautness of construction that recalls his early scores. The inventiveness of its successor is heard in the context of a conventional passacaglia, but equally notable is the appearance of the 12th century *Hymn to St. Magnus,* alongside a related 14th century plainsong. Both had previously been used in *Hymn to St. Magnus,* for soprano and ensemble, and it is tempting to speculate that they may provide the basic material for the new project.

Hardly less significant has been Max's return to works for chorus and orchestra after more than 30 years. Again, the catalyst was Mackay Brown, whose poetic text, based on the Christmas Story, Max had known for some years before incorporating it into his cantata, *The Three Kings.* He then gave the chorus a decisive role in *The Doctor of Myddfai,* his second full-scale opera, which can therefore be regarded as the true sequel of *Taverner.* As in the earlier opera, there are parallels between the compositional procedures and the drama, in which the roles of the main protagonists are transformed. Both works have an important political dimension, but whereas *Taverner* belongs to the past and deals with religious superstition, *The Doctor of Myddfai* offers a vision of the near future, based on current fears of a mysterious disease.

In many ways, the oratorio, *Job,* can be regarded as an extension of the choral writing in *The Doctor of Myddfai.* The techniques of characterisation and dramatisation are much the same as in the opera, and the chorus fulfils many functions, along with the orchestra and the four soloists. Consequently, the oratorio's expressive potential is hardly diminished by the absence of theatrical apparatus, and Max's preoccupation with largescale choral works may explain his statement that *The Doctor of Myddfai* is likely to be his last full-scale opera.

Finally, a brief look at the lighter music, which ranges from transcriptions of renaissance and baroque pieces to unashamedly popular scores. Max's wind-up gramophone, which remains an essential household item, is symbolic of his long-standing identification with popular styles. It enabled him to play old records of the foxtrots he first encountered during the war, and which manifested themselves in such pieces as *St. Thomas Wake,* or his transcription of Purcell's *Fantasia* and *Two Pavans.* In the

late 1960s, foxtrots reflected Max's preoccupation with parody, but the emphasis changed to humour with music for Ken Russell's film of the Sandy Wilson musical, *The Boyfriend.* In more recent pieces, of which the best-known is probably *An Orkney Wedding, with Sunrise,* foxtrots have tended to be replaced by Scottish, or Orcadian folk dance, but material from American popular culture has also been used in *Mavis in Las Vegas.*

Max's light music undoubtedly serves as a form of relaxation from more ambitious scores. It is also designed to question the widely held view that composers should concentrate exclusively on creating 'masterpieces'. Above all, it is often functional music, frequently associated with some form of celebration. As such, it fits in with Max's idea that the arts should serve a useful purpose within society. Max's move from Hoy to the island of Sanday has already been marked by a set of children's songs, which was heard at the 1999 St. Magnus Festival, and it may also have provoked a degree of stocktaking.

Since the last update, several major works have reached fruition, bringing Max ever closer to his ambition of concentrating almost exclusively on his cycle of ten string quartets. May and June 2000 were particularly important, with four outstanding premieres.

On 2 May 2000, in an all-Max programme conducted by the composer, the Royal Philharmonic Orchestra (RPO) gave the first performances of the *Horn Concerto,* with Richard Watkins as soloist, and *Roma, Amor, Labyrinthos.* The *Horn Concerto* brought to a spectacular conclusion a sequence of solo concertos with which the RPO has been associated, while *Roma, Amor, Labyrinthos,* inspired by Max's frequent visits to Rome, belongs to a series of symphonic works with programmatic elements. *The Antarctic Symphony (Symphony No. 8),* which will be premiered on 6 May 2001 by the Philharmonia Orchestra with subsequent performances in the same week in Leicester and at the Brighton Festival, and again at the St. Magnus Festival in June by the BBC Scottish Symphony Orchestra, also falls into this category, rather than to the cycle of more conventional symphonies, completed with *Symphony No. 7* at last year's St. Magnus Festival.

Whereas the seventh symphony reflects a compositional 'journey', the *Antarctic Symphony* has been stimulated by a visit to the

Antarctic itself sponsored by BAS, which was one of the terms of the commission. Accordingly, the work is partly a sonic representation of Max's experiences, including the icebreaker ship's encounters with the frozen sea, the immense stillness of the frozen landscape, and the peculiar quality of the light, which makes very distant objects seem remarkably close. Above all, the temporal dimension will be a significant feature of what may prove to be Max's last major orchestral score.

Likewise, *Mr. Emmet Takes a Walk,* also introduced at the 24th St. Magnus Festival, was his final contribution to music theatre, and *Canticum Canticorum,* for soloists, chorus and orchestra, to be given its first performance at the International Organ Festival in Nuremberg in July, will be the last of several choral works he has written in recent years. This will be a substantial score, lasting about 45 minutes, and will be larger than two other commissions for the Danish ensemble Athelas, and the City of London Sinfonia.

Yet although Max will fulfil all his commitments before embarking on his quartet cycle, the switch of emphasis towards chamber music has already resulted in two recent additions to the *Trumpet Quintet* he finished two years ago. He composed a fanfare for two trumpets for the International Trumpet Guild called *Fanfare for Lowry* (The Lowry Centre being the new Arts Complex recently opened in Salford, very close to the place where Max was born), and an eight-minute String Trio, called *Dove, Star-Folded,* in memory of Sir Steven Runciman. A solo piece for double-bass and Duncan McTier (for whom he wrote the *Strathclyde Concerto No. 7* for Double Bass) is scheduled for the forthcoming St. Magnus Festival.

From this, it is apparent that Max's string quartets are likely to generate a number of satellite works for various chamber music combinations. It may therefore be assumed that his output over the next few years will not merely enrich the quartet repertoire, but the entire range of chamber music.

Chronological list of published works
This is a complete chronological list of all Sir Peter Maxwell Davies' published works.

All dates shown are completion dates of the composition.

1952	*Quartet Movement.* For string quartet. Published by Chester Music.
1955	*Sonata for Trumpet.* For trumpet and piano. Published by Schott.
1956	*Five Pieces for Piano.* For piano solo. Published by Schott.
1956	*Stedman Doubles (1956, rev. 1968).* For clarinet and percussion. Published by Boosey & Hawkes.
1956	*Clarinet Sonata.* For clarinet and piano. Published by Chester Music.
1957	*Alma Redemptoris Mater.* For wind sextet. Published by Schott.
1957	*St. Michael.* Sonata for 17 wind instruments. Published by Schott.
1958	*Prolation.* For orchestra. Published by Schott.
1958	*Stedman Caters (1958 rev. 1968).* For instrumental ensemble. Published by Boosey & Hawkes.
1959	*Ricercar and Doubles.* On 'To many a Well' for instrumental ensemble. Published by Schott.
1959	*William Byrd: Three Dances.* Arranged for school orchestra. Published by Schott.
1959	*Five Motets.* For SATB chorus, SATB solo and instrumental ensemble. Published by Boosey & Hawkes.
1959	*Five Klee Pictures (1959, rev. 1976).* For school orchestra. Published by Boosey & Hawkes.
1960	*Organ Fantasia from O Magnum Mysterium.* For organ solo. Published by Schott.
1960	*O Magnum Mysterium.* Four carols for SATB chorus, with two instrumental sonatas and organ fantasia. Published by Schott.
1960	*Five Voluntaries.* Arrangements of voluntaries by William Croft, Jeremiah Clarke, Pierre Attaignant and Louis Couperin. Published by Schott.
1961	*String Quartet.* In one movement. Published by Schott.
1961	*Te Lucis Ante Terminum.* Compline hymn for SATB chorus and instrumental ensemble. Published by Schott.
1961	*Ave Maria, Hail Blessed Flower.* Carol for SATB chorus. Published by Novello.
1961	*Carol on St. Steven.* Carol for SATB chorus. Published by Schott.
1961	*Jesus Autem Hodie.* Carol for SATB chorus. Published by Schott.
1961	*Nowell.* Carol for SATB chorus. Published by Schott.
1961	*Alma Redemptoris Mater.* Carol for four equal voices. Published by Schott.
1962	*Sinfonia.* For orchestra. Published by Schott.
1962	*The Lord's Prayer.* For SATB chorus. Published by Schott.
1962	*Leopardi Fragments.* Cantata for soprano, contralto and instrumental ensemble. Published by Schott.
1962	*First Fantasia on an 'In Nomine' of John Taverner.* For orchestra. Published by Schott.
1963	*Veni Sancte Spiritus.* For SATB chorus, SATB soli and orchestra. Published by Boosey & Hawkes.
1964	*Second Fantasia on John Taverner's 'In Nomine'.* For orchestra. Published by Boosey & Hawkes.
1964	*Shakespeare Music.* For instrumental ensemble. Published by Boosey & Hawkes.
1964	*Ave, Plena Gracia.* Carol for SATB chorus, with optional organ. Published by Oxford University Press.
1964	*Five Little Pieces for Piano.* For piano solo. Published by Boosey & Hawkes.
1965	*The Shepherds' Calendar.* For SATB youth chorus and instruments. Published by Boosey & Hawkes.
1965	*Seven In Nomine.* For instrumental ensemble. Published by Boosey & Hawkes.
1965	*Ecce Manus Tradentis.* Motet for SATB chorus, SATB soli and instrumental ensemble. Published by Boosey & Hawkes.
1965	*Revelation and Fall.* Monodrama for soprano and instrumental ensemble. Published by Boosey & Hawkes.
1965	*Shall I Die for Mannis Sake?* Carol for SA chorus and piano. Published by Boosey & Hawkes.
1966	*Notre Dame des Fleurs.* Music-theatre work for soprano, mezzo-soprano, countertenor and instrumental ensemble. Published by Chester Music.
1966	*Five Carols.* For SAA chorus. Published by Boosey & Hawkes.
1967	*Antechrist.* For instrumental ensemble. Published by Boosey & Hawkes.
1967	*Hymnos.* For clarinet and piano. Published by Boosey & Hawkes.
1968	*Missa super L'Homme Armé (1968, rev. 1971).* Parody mass for speaker or singer (male or female) and instrumental ensemble. Published by Boosey & Hawkes.
1968	*Stedman Caters (1958, rev. 1968).* For instrumental ensemble. Published by Boosey & Hawkes.
1968	*Purcell: Fantasia and Two Pavans.* Realisation for instrumental ensemble. Published by Boosey & Hawkes.
1969	*St. Thomas Wake.* Foxtrot for orchestra on a Pavan by John Bull. Published by Boosey & Hawkes.
1969	*Worldes Blis.* For orchestra. Published by Boosey & Hawkes.
1969	*Eight Songs for a Mad King.* Music-theatre work for male voice and instrumental ensemble. Published by Boosey & Hawkes.
1969	*Solita.* For flute solo. Published by Boosey & Hawkes.
1969	*Gabrieli: Canzona.* Realisation for small chamber orchestra or for instrumental ensemble. Published by Chester Music.
1969	*Vesalii Icones.* Music-theatre work for dancer, solo cello and instrumental ensemble. Published by Boosey & Hawkes.
1969	*Sub Tuam Protectionem.* For piano solo. Published by Chester Music.
1970	*Taverner.* Opera in two acts. Published by Boosey & Hawkes.

1970 *Points and Dances from Taverner.*
Instrumental dances and keyboard pieces from the opera for instrumental ensemble.
Published by Boosey & Hawkes.

1970 *Ut Re Mi.*
For piano solo.
Published by Chester Music.

1970 *Buxtehude:*
'Also Hat Gott die Welt Geliebet'.
Cantata realisation for soprano and instrumental ensemble including 'original' interpretation.
Published by Chester Music.

1971 *From Stone to Thorn.*
Cantata for soprano and ensemble.
Published by Boosey & Hawkes.

1971 *Suite from The Devils.*
Drawn from the soundtrack of Ken Russell's film, for instrumental ensemble.
Published by Chester Music.

1971 *Suite from The Boyfriend.*
Drawn from the soundtrack of Ken Russell's film based on the musical by Sandy Wilson, for instrumental ensemble or for orchestra.
Published by Chester Music.

1971 *Canon in Memoriam Igor Stravinsky.*
Puzzle canon for instrumental ensemble.
Published by Boosey & Hawkes.

1972 *Blind Man's Buff.*
Masque.
Published by Chester Music.

1972 *Dunstable: Veni Sancte*
– Veni Creator Spiritus.
Realisation plus gloss for instrumental ensemble.
Published by Boosey & Hawkes.

1972 *Fool's Fanfare.*
For male speaker and instrumental ensemble.
Published by Chester Music.

1972 *Hymn to St. Magnus.*
For instrumental ensemble with mezzo-soprano obbligato.
Published by Boosey & Hawkes.

1972 *Tenebrae super Gesualdo.*
Motet with instrumental interpolations for SATB chorus and instrumental ensemble.
Published by Chester Music.

1972 *Lullaby for Ilian Rainbow.*
For guitar solo.
Published by Boosey & Hawkes.

1972 *J.S.Bach: Prelude and Fugue in C Sharp Minor.*
Realisation for instrumental ensemble.
Published by Boosey & Hawkes.

1973 *Stone Litany:*
Runes from a House of the Dead.
For mezzo-soprano and orchestra.
Published by Boosey & Hawkes.

1973 *Renaissance Scottish Dances.*
Arranged for instrumental ensemble.
Published by Boosey & Hawkes.

1973 *Si Quis Diligit Me.*
Motet on an original by David Peebles and Francy Heagy for instrumental ensemble.
Published by Boosey & Hawkes.

1973 *Purcell: Fantasia upon One Note.*
Realisation for instrumental ensemble.
Published by Chester Music.

1973 *Fiddlers at the Wedding.*
Song-cycle for mezzo-soprano and ensemble.
Published by Boosey & Hawkes.

1973 *Miss Donnithorne's Maggot.*
Music-theatre work for soprano or mezzo-soprano and instrumental ensemble.
Published by Boosey & Hawkes.

1973 *All Sons of Adam.*
Motet for instrumental ensemble on an anonymous 16th century Scottish original.
Published by Boosey & Hawkes.

1974 *Dark Angels.*
Song-cycle for mezzo-soprano and guitar.
Published by Boosey & Hawkes.

1974 *Psalm 124.*
Motet on early Scottish originals for instrumental ensemble.
Published by Boosey & Hawkes.

1974 *J.S.Bach: Prelude and Fugue in C Sharp Major.*
Realisation for instrumental ensemble.
Published by Boosey & Hawkes.

1975 *Ave Maris Stella.*
For instrumental ensemble.
Published by Boosey & Hawkes.

1975 *The Door of the Sun.*
For viola solo.
Published by Boosey & Hawkes.

1975 *The Kestrel Paced*
Round the Sun.
For flute solo.
Published by Boosey & Hawkes.

1975 *The Seven Brightnesses.*
For clarinet solo.
Published by Boosey & Hawkes.

1975 *Three Studies for Percussion.*
For eleven percussionists.
Published by Chester Music.

1975 *My Lady Lothian's Lilt.*
Realisation on an anonymous Scottish original for instrumental ensemble and mezzo-soprano obbligato.
Published by Boosey & Hawkes.

1975 *Stevie's Ferry to Hoy.*
For piano solo (beginners).
Published by Boosey & Hawkes.

1976 *Three Organ Voluntaries.*
For organ solo.
Published by Chester Music.

1976 *Kinloche his Fantassie.*
Realisation on a fantasy by 16th century Scottish composer William Kinloch, arranged for instrumental ensemble.
Published by Boosey & Hawkes.

1976 *Anakreontika.*
Song-cycle for mezzo-soprano and instrumental ensemble.
Published by Chester Music.

1976 *The Blind Fiddler.*
Song-cycle for mezzo-soprano and instrumental ensemble.
Published by Boosey & Hawkes.

1976 *Symphony No. 1.*
For orchestra.
Published by Boosey & Hawkes.

1976 *The Martyrdom of St. Magnus.*
Chamber opera in nine scenes.
Published by Boosey & Hawkes.

1976 *Ave Rex Angelorum.*
Carol for SATB chorus.
Published by Boosey & Hawkes.

1977 *A Mirror of Whitening Light.*
For instrumental ensemble.
Published by Boosey & Hawkes.

1977 *Westerlings.*
Four songs and a prayer, with seascapes for SATB chorus.
Published by Boosey & Hawkes.

1977 *Norn Pater Noster.*
Prayer for SATB chorus and organ.
Published by Boosey & Hawkes.

1977 *Runes from a Holy Island.*
For instrumental ensemble.
Published by Chester Music.

1977 *Little Quartet No. 2 (1977, rev. 1987).*
For string quartet.
Published by Boosey & Hawkes.

1977 *Our Father Whiche in Heaven Art.*
Motet on an original by John Angus for instrumental ensemble.
Published by Boosey & Hawkes.

1978 *The Two Fiddlers.*
Opera in two acts for young performers.
Published by Boosey & Hawkes.

1978 *Dances from The Two Fiddlers.*
Arranged for violin solo and instrumental ensemble.
Published by Boosey & Hawkes.

1978 *Le Jongleur de Notre Dame.*
Masque for mime-juggler, baritone, instrumental ensemble and children's band.
Published by Chester Music.

1978 *Salome.*
Ballet in two acts.
Published by Boosey & Hawkes.

1978 *Four Lessons.*
For two keyboard instruments.
Published by Boosey & Hawkes.

1979 *Black Pentecost.*
For mezzo-soprano, baritone and orchestra.
Published by Chester Music.

1979 *Solstice of Light.*
Cantata for tenor, SATB chorus and organ.
Published by Boosey & Hawkes.

1979 *Nocturne.*
For alto flute solo.
Published by Boosey & Hawkes.

1979 *Kirkwall Shopping Songs.*
Song-cycle for young children's voices and instruments.
Published by Boosey & Hawkes.

1979 *The Lighthouse.*
Chamber opera in one act with prologue.
Published by Chester Music.

1979 *Cinderella.*
Pantomime opera in two acts for young performers.
Published by Chester Music.

1980 *The Yellow Cake Revue.*
For singer or reciter and piano.
Published by Boosey & Hawkes.

1980 *Farewell to Stromness.*
Piano interlude from
The Yellow Cake Revue.
Published by Boosey & Hawkes.

1980 *Farewell to Stromness.*
Arranged for guitar by Timothy Walker.
Published by Boosey & Hawkes.

1980 *Yesnaby Ground.*
Piano interlude from
The Yellow Cake Revue.
Published by Boosey & Hawkes.

1980 *A Welcome to Orkney.*
For instrumental ensemble.
Published by Boosey & Hawkes.

1980 *Little Quartet No. 1.*
For string quartet.
Published by Boosey & Hawkes.

1980 *Symphony No. 2.*
For orchestra.
Published by Boosey & Hawkes.

1981 *The Medium Monodrama*
For mezzo-soprano solo.
Published by Boosey & Hawkes.

1981 *Piano Sonata.*
For piano solo.
Published by Chester Music.

1981 *The Rainbow.*
Music-theatre work for young performers.
Published by Chester Music.

1981 *Hill Runes.*
For guitar solo.
Published by Boosey & Hawkes.

1981 *The Bairns of Brugh.*
For instrumental ensemble.
Published by Boosey & Hawkes.

1981 *Sonatina for Trumpet.*
For trumpet solo.
Published by Boosey & Hawkes.

1981 *Lullaby for Lucy.*
For SATB chorus.
Published by Boosey & Hawkes.

1981 *Brass Quintet.*
Published by Chester Music.

1981 *Seven Songs Home.*
Song-cycle for children's voices.
Published by Chester Music.

1981 *Songs of Hoy.*
Song-cycle for children's voices and instruments.
Published by Chester Music.

1982 *Sea Eagle.*
For horn solo.
Published by Chester Music.

1982 *Image, Reflection, Shadow.*
For instrumental ensemble.
Published by Chester Music.

1982 *Sinfonia Concertante.*
For wind quintet and orchestra.
Published by Chester Music.

1982 *Organ Sonata.*
For organ solo.
Published by Chester Music.

1982 *Tallis: Four Voluntaries.*
Arranged for brass quintet.
Published by Chester Music.

1982 *Gesualdo: Two Motets.*
Arranged for brass quintet.
Published by Chester Music.

1982 *March: The Pole Star.*
For brass quintet.
Published by Chester Music.

1983 *Birthday Music for John.*
Trio for flute, viola and cello.
Published by Chester Music.

1983 *Into the Labyrinth.*
Cantata for tenor and orchestra.
Published by Chester Music.

1983 *Sinfonietta Accademica.*
For orchestra.
Published by Chester Music.

1984 *Agnus Dei.*
Motet for two solo sopranos, viola and cello.
Published by Chester Music.

1984 *Sonatina.*
For violin and cimbalom.
Published by Chester Music.

1984 *Unbroken Circle.*
For instrumental ensemble.
Published by Chester Music.

1984 *The No. 11 Bus.*
Music-theatre work for mime, singers, dancers and instrumental ensemble.
Published by Chester Music.

1984 *Guitar Sonata.*
For guitar solo.
Published by Chester Music.

1984 *One Star at Last.*
Carol for SATB chorus.
Published by Chester Music.

1984 *Symphony No. 3.*
For orchestra.
Published by Boosey & Hawkes.

1985 *An Orkney Wedding, with Sunrise.*
For orchestra.
Published by Boosey & Hawkes.

1985 *First Ferry to Hoy.*
For junior SATB chorus, junior percussion and recorder band and instrumental ensemble.
Published by Boosey & Hawkes.

1985 *The Peat Cutters.*
For SATB youth chorus, children's chorus and brass band.
Published by Boosey & Hawkes.

1985 *Concerto for Violin.*
For violin and orchestra.
Published by Chester Music.

1986 *Jimmack the Postie.*
Overture for orchestra.
Published by Chester Music.

1986 *House of Winter.*
Song-cycle for AATBBB chorus or vocal sextet.
Published by Chester Music.

1986 *Sea Runes.*
Song-cycle for vocal sextet or AATBBB chorus.
Published by Chester Music.

1986 *Excuse Me.*
Parlour songs, after Charles Dibdin, for mezzo-soprano and instrumental ensemble.
Published by Chester Music.

1986 *Winterfold.*
Song-cycle for mezzo-soprano and instrumental ensemble.
Published by Chester Music.

1986 *Dowland: Farewell a Fancye.*
Realisation for instrumental ensemble.
Published by Boosey & Hawkes.

1986 *Strathclyde Concerto No. 1.*
For oboe and orchestra.
Published by Boosey & Hawkes.

1987 *Resurrection.*
Opera in one act with prologue.
Published by Chester Music.

1987 *Strathclyde Concerto No. 2.*
For cello and orchestra.
Published by Chester Music.

1988 *Mishkenot.*
For instrumental ensemble.
Published by Boosey & Hawkes.

1988 *Concerto for Trumpet.*
For trumpet and orchestra.
Published by Boosey & Hawkes.

1988 *Dances from The Two Fiddlers.*
Arranged for violin and piano.
Published by Boosey & Hawkes.

1988 *Six Songs for St. Andrews.*
Song-cycle for young children's
voices and instruments.
Published by Chester Music.

1989 *The Great Bank Robbery.*
Music-theatre work for young
performers.
Published by Chester Music.

1989 *Symphony No. 4.*
For orchestra.
Published by Boosey & Hawkes.

1989 *Hallelujah!
The Lord God Almightie.*
For SATB chorus,
SA semichorus (or soli)
and organ.
Published by Chester Music.

1989 *Jupiter Landing.*
Music-theatre work for young
performers.
Published by Chester Music.

1989 *Strathclyde Concerto No. 3.*
For horn, trumpet and orchestra.
Published by Boosey & Hawkes.

1989 *Dinosaur at Large.*
Music-theatre work for young
performers.
Published by Chester Music.

1989 *Threnody on a Plainsong for
Michael Vyner.*
For orchestra.
Published by Chester Music.

1990 *Dangerous Errand.*
Music-theatre work for very
young performers.
Published by Chester Music.

1990 *Strathclyde Concerto No. 4.*
For clarinet and orchestra.
Published by Chester Music.

1990 *Caroline Mathilde.*
Ballet in two acts.
Published by Chester Music.

1990 *Apple Basket: Apple Blossom.*
For SATB chorus.
Published by Chester Music.

1990 *Hymn to the Word of God.*
Motet for SATB chorus and
tenor soli.
Published by Chester Music.

1991 *Ojai Festival Overture.*
For orchestra.
Published by Boosey & Hawkes.

1991 *The Spiders' Revenge.*
Music-theatre work for young
performers.
Published by Chester Music.

1991 *Caroline Mathilde:
Concert Suite from Act I
of the Ballet.*
For orchestra.
Published by Chester Music.

1991 *Strathclyde Concerto No. 5.*
For violin, viola and string
orchestra.
Published by Boosey & Hawkes.

1991 *Ban: Vanitas.*
Arranged for string orchestra.
Published by Boosey & Hawkes.

1991 *Strathclyde Concerto No. 6.*
For flute and orchestra.
Published by Chester Music.

1991 *First Grace of Light.*
For oboe solo.
Published by Boosey & Hawkes.

1991 *Caroline Mathilde: Concert Suite
from Act II of the Ballet.*
For orchestra.
Published by Chester Music.

1992 *A Selkie Tale.*
Music-theatre work for young
performers.
Published by Chester Music.

1992 *The Turn of the Tide.*
For orchestra and children's
chorus and young
instrumentalists/composers.
Published by Chester Music.

1992 *Strathclyde Concerto No. 7.*
For double bass and orchestra.
Published by Chester Music.

1992 *Sir Charles his Pavan.*
For orchestra.
Published by Schott.

1993 *Seven Summer Songs.*
Song-cycle for young children's
voices and instruments.
Published by Chester Music.

1993 *Strathclyde Concerto No. 8.*
For bassoon and orchestra.
Published by Chester Music.

1993 *Two Dances from Caroline Mathilde.*
Arranged for flute and harp.
Published by Chester Music.

1993 *Corpus Christi,
with Cat and Mouse.*
For SATB chorus.
Published by Chester Music.

1993 *A Spell for Green Corn:
The MacDonald Dances.*
For violin and orchestra.
Published by Chester Music.

1993 *Six Secret Songs.*
For piano solo.
Published by Chester Music.

1993 *Shepherds of Hoy.*
Carol for young children's voices
and piano.
Published by Chester Music.

1993 *Chat Moss.*
For school orchestra.
Published by Chester Music.

1994 *A Hoy Calendar.*
For SATB chorus.
Published by Chester Music.

1994 *Symphony No. 5.*
For orchestra.
Published by Boosey & Hawkes.

1994 *Cross Lane Fair.*
For Northumbrian pipes and
orchestra.
Published by Chester Music.

1994 *Carolísima.*
Serenade for chamber orchestra
or instrumental ensemble.
Published by Schott.

1994 *Mercurius.*
For SATB chorus and crotales.
Published by Chester Music.

1994 *Strathclyde Concerto No. 9.*
For six woodwind instruments
and string orchestra.
Published by Chester Music.

1995 *The Beltane Fire.*
Choreographic poem for orchestra.
Published by Boosey & Hawkes.

1995 *Time and the Raven.*
For orchestra.
Published by Chester Music.

1995 *Thaw.*
For instrumental ensemble.
Published by Boosey & Hawkes.

1995 *The Three Kings.*
For SATB Soli, SATB chorus
and orchestra.
Published by Chester Music.

1995 *The Doctor of Myddfai.*
Opera in two acts.
Published by Boosey & Hawkes.

1996 *Symphony No. 6.*
For orchestra.
Published by Boosey & Hawkes.

1996 *Reliqui Domum Meum.*
For solo organ.
Published by Chester Music.

1996 *A Birthday Card for Hans.*
For mezzo-soprano and
instrumental ensemble.
Published by Schott.

1996 *Strathclyde Concerto No. 10.*
Concerto for orchestra.
Published by Boosey & Hawkes.

1996 *Throstle's Nest Junction.*
For orchestra.
Published by Chester Music.

1996 *Piccolo Concerto.*
For piccolo and orchestra.
Published by Chester Music.

1996 *Job.*
Oratorio for SATB Soli, SATB
chorus and orchestra.
Published by Chester Music.

1996 *Mavis in Las Vegas.*
Theme and variations for orchestra.
Published by Chester Music.

1996 *Orkney Saga I: (formerly Sails in
St. Magnus I) Fifteen keels laid in
Norway for Jerusalem-farers.*
For orchestra.
Published by Boosey & Hawkes.

1996 *Il Rozzo Martello.*
For unaccompanied SATB chorus.
Published by Chester Music.

1996 *The Jacobite Rising.*
For SATB Soli, SATB chorus
and orchestra.
Published by Chester Music.

1996 *Piano Concerto.*
For piano and orchestra.
Published by Chester Music.

1996 *Orkney Saga II: (formerly Sails in
St. Magnus II) In Kirkwall,
the first red Saint Magnus Stones.*
For orchestra.
Published by Boosey & Hawkes.

1998 *A Reel of Seven Fishermen.*
For orchestra.
Published by Boosey & Hawkes.

1998 *An Orkney Tune.*
For piano solo – beginners.
Published by MaxOpus.

1998 *Maxwell's Reel, with Northern Lights.*
For orchestra.
Published by Chester Music.

1998 *Mrs. Linklater's Tune.*
For violin solo.
Published by Chester Music.

1998 *Sea Elegy.*
For SATB Soli, SATB chorus
and orchestra.
Published by Chester Music.

1998 *Roma Amor Labyrinthos.*
For orchestra.
Published by Chester Music.

1998 *Fanfare.*
For brass ensemble.
Published by Chester Music.

1998 *Swinton Jig.*
For orchestra.
Published by Chester Music.

1998 *Temenos with Mermaids and Angels.*
For flute and orchestra.
Published by Chester Music.

1999 *Orkney Saga III:
(formerly Sails in St. Magnus III)
An Orkney wintering.
Stone poems in Orkahowe:
"great treasure...".*
For saxophone and orchestra.
Published by Boosey & Hawkes.

1999 *Trumpet Quintet.*
For trumpet and string quartet.
Published by Chester Music.

1999 *Litany – for a Ruined Chapel
between Sheep and Shore.*
For trumpet solo.
Published by Chester Music.

1999 *Spinning Jenny.*
Concert overture for orchestra.
Published by Chester Music.

1999 *Jubilate Deo.*
For chorus and organ with brass
ensemble.
Published by Schott.

1999 *High on the Slopes of Terror.*
For orchestra.
Published by Boosey & Hawkes.

1999 *Mr. Emmet Takes a Walk.*
Music-theatre work for soprano,
baritone, bass and instrumental
ensemble.
Published by Boosey & Hawkes.

1999 *Horn Concerto.*
For horn and orchestra.
Published by Chester Music.

2000 *Fanfare for Lowry.*
For two solo trumpets.
Published by Boosey & Hawkes.

2000 *Orkney Saga V: (formerly Sails in
St. Magnus V) Westerly Gale in
Biscay, Salt in the Bread Broken.*
For SATB chorus and orchestra.
Published by Boosey & Hawkes.

2000 *Symphony No. 7.*
For orchestra.
Published by Boosey & Hawkes.

2000 *A Dream of Snow.*
For SSAA children's chorus.
Published by Chester Music.

2000 *Una Balena Azzurra.*
For SATBB Chorus, with optional
organ or piano accompaniment.
Published by Chester Music.

2000 *Antarctic Symphony (Symphony No. 8).*
For orchestra.
Published by Boosey & Hawkes.

2001 *Dove, Star-Folded.*
For string trio.
Published by MaxOpus.

2001 *Canticum Canticorum.*
For SATB soli, SATB chorus and
orchestra.
Published by Chester Music.

Sir Peter Maxwell Davies
Curriculum vitae

1934	Born Salford, 8 September, son of Thomas and Hilda Davies.
1945-53	Leigh Grammar School.
1953-56	Royal Manchester College of Music.
1953-56	Manchester University.
1956	Mus B(Hons).
1957-58	Studied with Goffredo Petrassi in Rome.
1959-62	Director of Music, Cirencester Grammar School.
1962-64	Harkness Fellowship, Graduate School, Princeton University. Studied with Roger Sessions, Milton Babbitt, Earl Kim.
1967-71	Founder and co-director with Harrison Birtwistle of The Pierrot Players.
1970	First visit to Orkney.
1971	Went to live in Orkney.
1971-87	Founder and Artistic Director of The Fires of London.
1977-86	Founder and Artistic Director of the St. Magnus Festival, Orkney Islands.
1978	Fellow of the Royal Northern College of Music.
1979	Honorary Member of the Royal Academy of Music.
1979	Member of the Accademica Filarmonia Romana.
1979	Honorary Doctor of Music, Edinburgh University.
1979-84	Artistic Director, Dartington Summer School of Music.
1981	Honorary Doctor of Law, Aberdeen University.
1981	Honorary Member of the Guildhall School of Music and Drama.
1981	Commander of the British Empire, Queen's Birthday Honours.
1981	Honorary Doctor of Music, Manchester University.
1983-	President, Schools Music Association.
1984	Honorary Doctor of Music, Bristol University.
1985	President, North of England Education Conference (Chester).
1985	Visiting Fromm Professor of Composition, Harvard University.
1985-94	Associate Composer/Conductor, Scottish Chamber Orchestra.
1986-	President, Composers' Guild of Great Britain.
1986-	President, St. Magnus Festival, Orkney Islands.
1986	Honorary Doctor of Music, Open University.
1986	Honorary Doctor of Letters, University of Warwick.
1987	Knight Bachelor, New Year's Honours, for services to music.
1987	Honorary Member of the Royal Philharmonic Society.
1988	L'Officier dans L'Ordre des Arts et des Lettres.
1989-	President, National Federation of Music Societies.
1989	Cobbett Medal for services to chamber music.
1991	First Award of the Association of British Orchestras for outstanding contribution to the benefit of orchestras and promotion of orchestral life in the UK.
1991	Gulliver Award for the Performing Arts in Scotland for outstanding contribution to the performing arts in Scotland.
1992	Portrait painted by John Bellany for the Royal Scottish Portrait Gallery in Edinburgh.
1992-00	Conductor/Composer, BBC Philharmonic.
1992-00	Associate Conductor/Composer of the Royal Philharmonic Orchestra.
1993	Honorary Doctor of Music, Glasgow University.
1993	Member of the Royal Swedish Academy of Music.
1993	Archive of the autograph manuscripts and sketches purchased by the British Library.
1994-97	President, Cheltenham Arts Festivals.
1994	Honorary Fellow of the Royal Incorporation of Architects in Scotland.
1994	Fellow of the Royal Scottish Academy of Music and Drama.
1994-	Composer Laureate, Scottish Chamber Orchestra.
1994	Fellow, Royal College of Music, London.
1994	Honorary Doctor of Music, Durham University.
1995	National Federation of Music Societies, Charles Groves Award for outstanding contribution to British music.
1995	Royal Philharmonic Society Award for Large-Scale Composition for *Symphony No. 5*.
1995-	President, Society for the Promotion of New Music.
1998	Portrait, Royal College of Music, London.
1998	Elected a member of the Bayerische Akademie der Schönen Künste, Munich.
1999	Honorary Doctor of Music, University of Salford.
2001	Honorary Doctor of Music, University of Hull.
2001	Honorary Member of the Royal Scottish Society.

Notes from a Cold Climate

Antarctic Symphony (Symphony No. 8)

Notes from a Cold Climate

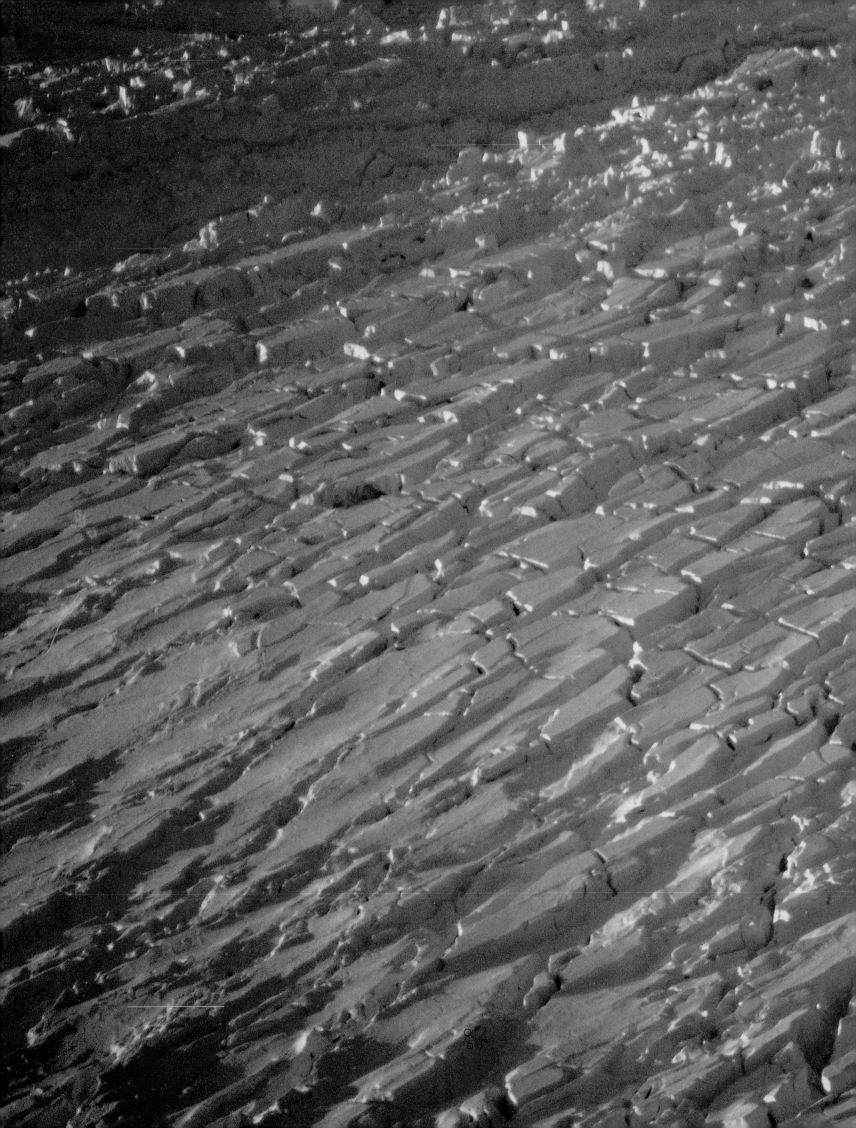